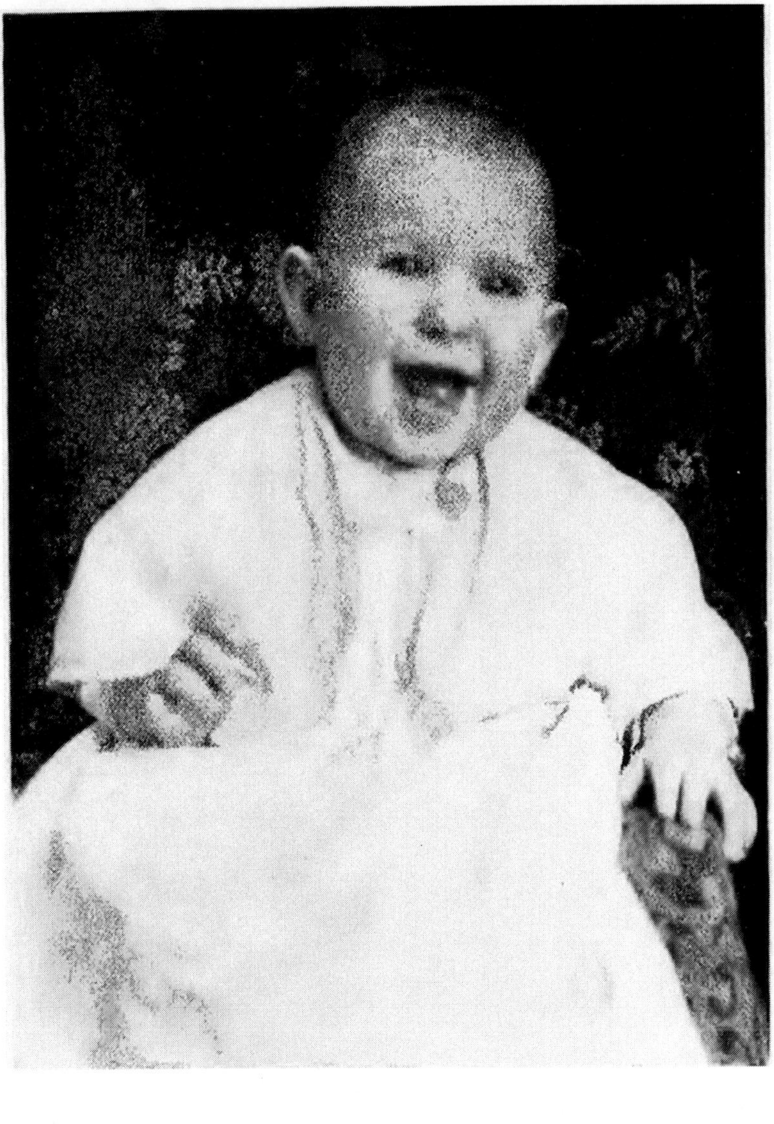

WARREN ED WARD MORRIS

Not a Ranger - At present commanding officer over all around him. A nephew of W. J . L. Sullivan. Son of Mr. and Mrs. Edward_S. Morris, of Carthage, Texas.

TWELVE YEARS IN THE SADDLE FOR LAW AND ORDER

ON THE

FRONTIERS OF TEXAS

BY

SERGEANT W. J. L. SULLIVAN

Texas Ranger

CO. B, FRONTIER BATTALION

GYAN

ISBN : 978-81-212-9016-6 (HB)

First Published, 1909

Indian Reprintg in 2017

Published by

Gyan Publishing House
5, Ansari Road
Daryaganj, New Delhi-110002
Phone: 9811692060
E-mail: books@gyanbooks.com

Printed at: G. Print Process, Delhi.

CONTENTS

POEMS

LIST OF ILLUSTRATIONS

PREFATORY

In offering this book to the public, I have not undertaken to present a history of my life. I do not consider my life of enough importance to warrant making a book about it. What I have undertaken to do is to tell some of the exciting experiences that have fallen to the lot of that noble band, the Texas Ranger force, of which I had the honor to be a member for twelve years. I had the leading part, it is true, in the incidents related, but the reader will see that I was not the whole show—there were others. I have prefixed some brief notes concerning my ancestry, and some incidents of my youth, and have followed with true accounts, written in my own plain way, of the principal events of my career as a Sergeant of the Rangers.

I have introduced plates herein, made from photographs, showing the faces of some of the most noted criminals in the annals of Texas; also photo illustrations of some of my dear comrades—all of them, in fact, that I could procure for this edition of my book. In a future edition, I will probably be able to add the likenesses of others.

For valuable assistance in the preparation of these pages, I am indebted to numerous friends, who I will not enumerate by name, but whose kindness will ever be remembered by me. I solicit their continued help, and will appreciate suggestions that may be made by these and other friends and patriotic Texans in general, for use in a contemplated future edition of this work.

With a respectful bow to my audience—the public—and a plea for their indulgence instead of their exacting criticism, I am,

Very cordially, The Author,

W. J. L. SULLIVAN.

ERRATA

Page 79, third line from bottom of first paragraph, should read "when I *heard* him make this remark," instead of "when I *made* him make this remark."

Page 110, seventh line on the page, should read "Just *after* we entered the house," instead of "Just *before* we entered the house."

MY ANCESTRY.

My father, Tom Sullivan, was born and raised at No. 99 Broome Street, New York City, where he engaged in business as a master mechanic. My grandfather, John Sullivan, was born in Ireland. He and my grandmother moved to New York City and settled on Broome Street, where my father, who was an only child, was born. My grandfather was a Mason by order and also by occupation. Just before my father's death my grandfather wrote him that he was coming to him to bring him fifteen hundred dollars that he had collected from the rents of my father's property, which was in the City of New York. He started out with the money, as he said he would, and has never been heard of up to seven years ago, when a bank book of his was found in a savings bank in New York.

My father went to Perry County, Alabama, and met and married my mother, Summer McFarlen, and they moved to Winston County, Mississippi, where my father engaged in farming until his death.

I

A Runaway

I was born in Winston County, Mississippi, on the 10th day of July, in 1851. My father had died seventy-nine days before my birth, leaving my mother with three other children besides me. Later on my m o t h e r married a Mr. Presley, of Leek County, and two children were born to them. My stepfather moved with us to Bradley County, Arkansas, where my mother died when I was but eight years of age.

My stepfather married again. That left me, as it proved to be, in a bad predicament. I had no father nor mother, and my stepfather, after my mother's death, had married another woman. My only sister also married, and soon after that my brother, Tom, died, which left my other brother, Jim, and me to take care of ourselves as best we could. Our troubles had only begun, however, for in 1861 the Civil War broke out, and my stepfather, Mr. Presley, and my brother-in-law went to the front, where both were killed, fighting for the cause of the Confederacy. When Presley went to the war he left Jim and me with his father-in-law, a Mr. Jeams. It was a cruel fate for us to meet. "Old man Jeams," as he was commonly called, was very hard on Jim and me. A merciless tyrant, with no feeling or principle, he beat us many times until we were so stunned and stupefied that we could not realize whether we were dead or alive. It is a terrible thing for poor, little, innocent children to fall into the tight, greedy clutches of such a man as this.

Jeams was known all over that section of the country as a hard character, and the soldiers stationed in that vicinity learned how brutal he was to my brother and me and paid him a visit one night, about two o'clock, to adjust matters with him with the aid of a new rope, which one of the men carried for convenience on the horn of his saddle. There were about twenty-five in the party, and they called Jeams out to the gate for an interview. One man in the squad, a Mr. Bloxom, had a greater grudge than the others against Jeams; for the latter had stolen a fine milk cow from Bloxom's widowed daughter, of which fact Bloxom had informed the others of the party. After getting Jeams out of the house, they asked him where the two little boys were, who lived with him. Jeams answered that they were in bed. They then told him to rouse us and bring us to the gate, which he promptly did. They asked us if we were living with "old man Jonathan Jeams." We told them that we were. Then they asked us if our stepfather and brother-in-law were not fighting in the war. We answered that they were. The soldiers then asked us if it was not true that Jeams beat and abused us a great deal. They immediately followed that question up with other inquiries as to the manner in which we were generally mistreated by our stepfather's father-in-law. Brother Jim was afraid to tell them the truth, for fear his guardian would make it all the harder for him in the future, so he denied that he was mistreated, and said that Jeams was good to us.

I spoke up when Jim got through and told the soldiers that my brother was afraid to tell the truth; that Jeams whipped and abused us all the time, and that occasionally he would beat us nearly to death. Jim contradicted the things that I told them, but the soldiers said that if his story had corroborated mine, they would break Jeams' neck right there with their rope. This talk, however, frightened Jim all the more, and when they asked him again if "Old Jeams" wasn't making slaves of us, he vigorously denied it. They asked Jim if Jeams had stolen the cow that belonged to Bloxom's daughter, but Jim got further from the truth than ever, and denied that too. I knew that Jeams had stolen the cow and killed her for beef, and I told the soldiers that; but the statements that Jim and I had made were conflicting, and the soldiers would not hang him.

They still believed Jeams to be guilty, however, and lectured him about an hour and a half before they let him go to bed. They told him they would watch him after that, and see that he conducted himself properly as long as he lived in that community. Jim and I went back to bed, but could sleep no more the rest of the night for thinking over this exciting episode.

If Jim had not been so frightened, and had borne me out in my statements, the soldiers would have hung Jeams, and from that hour we would have been entirely and forever free from that heartless tyrant; but, as it was, we lay in our bed the remainder of that eventful night, debating, in whispers, as to whether the soldiers' visit, since it resulted as it did, would make our life more pleasant or more miserable. Since Jeams had heard what I had to say to the soldiers, and since he was permitted to live on guard over me, I decided that he was going to make things even more disagreeable for me, if possible, than ever before; so I told my brother that I was going to make my escape the next day if I got a chance.

I knew that the sooner I got off the better, so at twelve o'clock I bade my brother good-bye, climbed over the fence behind the barn, and hit the trail like a deer. I ran as swiftly as my legs could carry me, and jumped over logs and bushes to save the time it would take to go around them. A few times I looked back just long enough to see if I was being pursued; then I would run faster than ever on my way to Mr. Bloxom, the man whose daughter's cow was stolen by Jeams. I enjoyed the prospects of getting out of Jeams' reach. If I had not run away from him, he would have made a "ship-wreck" of me for telling the soldiers about his lawlessness. Soon I, myself, was to be with those soldiers, and to have their protection, and I was glad.

When I reached Bloxom's home he saluted me, and told me that I had done right, and asked me where my brother was. I told him that he was still in Jeams' hands. Bloxom then took occasion to remark that Jeams would have been a dead man, if my brother's story had not conflicted with the statements which I had made the night before. I asked Mr. Bloxom if he thought I could stay with the soldiers. He assured me that I could, and got his son, Tom, to saddle his horse and take me over to Carter's regiment. I rode behind Tom, and we reached the soldiers' camp some time after dark.

Jeams guessed that I had gone to Bloxom's and put my brother on a mule and sent him over there in search of me. Bloxom advised him to join me and stay with the army. Jim told him that he couldn't do that, as he had the "old man's" mule, and that he had to go back on that account. Bloxom sent the mule back to Jeams by a soldier, and some one conducted Jim to the regiment where I had gone, he reaching camp an hour or two after I did. Jim was afraid to run away, but felt mightily relieved when the soldiers took us with them and gave us their protection.

II

BETTER DAYS

Never shall I forget the night that Brother and I reached the soldiers' camp, when we first joined Carter's regiment. Everything seemed very different from what we were used to, but we felt easier and more comfortable. We were not afraid that we would be jerked up at any moment and cuffed about and abused, as was Jeams' manner of treating us. The soldiers felt sorry for Jim and me and treated us as kindly as they could. Col. Giddings had charge of this regiment, and knowing the plight we were in told us that we could stay with his men as long as we wished. We were too young to fight, but we began to feel as if we were real soldiers. Once, while we were with the regiment, the soldiers captured, somewhere on the Arkansas River, four hundred mules, one hundred and twenty-five or thirty wagons, and several Yankees. At another place, we captured about three hundred beeves.

We had been with the regiment about fifteen months, when three of the soldiers, Trave Burton, Bill Henley and Leonard Burns, got furloughs to go home. This was about two months before the close of the war. The three men asked Brother Jim and me to go home with them. We accepted their kind invitation, and with them left the army. For a little while I lived with Leonard Burns, and James stayed with Trave Burton. Later on, however, we got together, and both of us lived with Mr.

and Mrs. Bill Henley, with whom we stayed for a number of years, not leaving them until we were about grown.

Mr. and Mrs. Henley were like father and mother to James and me. I never knew before what it was to be in such a good home. It seemed a paradise to me, who had been left an orphan boy, unprotected, and at the mercy of rough, careless, unfeeling people, and I could well appreciate my new surroundings. It is sad for little children to be left without a father and mother to take care of them, and when poor, little orphans endure what James and I had to bear, they should be very thankful when they are placed in a good home, as we were. God pity the orphan children of this world, and may He bless the kind-hearted people who take them in and raise them to become useful men and women.

Mr. and Mrs. Henley always taught and encouraged us to be honest and industrious, and to have a proper regard for the law. Through respect for their memory, and because I owed it to myself and to my own father and mother who died in my infancy, I always lived up to those teachings. Since I have served the people of Texas as a ranger and dealt with numerous criminals, I have learned through personal observation, the wisdom of the teachings of those good old people. The world is full of tragedies, and, having been a state officer for over twelve years, I have witnessed many of them myself. Many criminals have brought shame, misery and trouble upon themselves, their families and their friends, because they started out in their youth with no respect for the laws of God and man. In the following chapters I shall tell you the tragic story of dozens of criminals who wound up their careers in the penitentiary—or, in a few instances, at the rope's end.

In some cases the men had no parents, while children, to care for them, nor any one else to teach them how to become honest, upright and useful. In other cases, however, they were men who had parents, but, while young and "smart," had disregarded the teachings of their elders, and, later on, had flagrantly violated the laws of their country, until they were finally locked within the four walls of a penitentiary, their liberty gone, and themselves disgraced and despised. They are left in dark, lonely cells to brood day and night over their unhappy fate, and to realize the folly of their former misbehavior.

I have encountered many men who appeared, at first sight, to be good, but who were really tough characters, and who, unfortunaltey, possessed much influence for evil over their companions. Thus, young people should be very careful with whom they associate. I have, also, seen men in good circumstances disobey the law for some material acquisition, and lose whatever they had thereby gained, together with all they ever possessed before, trying to stave off the prosecution; and they were fortunate, even at that, if they are not finally sent to the penitentiary. With these impressive lessons before me, and because I ever wanted to do my duty and be honest, thereby gaining my own self-respect, I always tried to do what I thought was right, and I respected and obeyed the laws of my country. Once or twice, when I was young, I laid wagers with money, and several times I drank whiskey; but I soon saw the folly in these, the only vicious habits that I ever started, and nipped them in the bud. For twelve years my business took me into the worst saloons, gambling dens, and low dives in Texas, but I always managed to keep from falling into the habits of the people whom I encountered in these places.

I am getting old now, and, as people usually do in their declining years, I spend many of my idle hours in meditation, thinking ever of the incidents of my past life; and, while thus reviewing my record as an officer and an honest citizen, I am rewarded with the only genuine happiness and satisfaction that man can experience while, with tottering footsteps, he is nearing the gateway through which he passes into the unknown world beyond.

III

AN INDIAN RAID

In 1871 I joined a party of cattlemen who were on their way to Ellsworth, Kansas, to which place they were driving three thousand head of cattle, which belonged to Tom Pullman and a Mr. Matthews. These two gentlemen owned three more herds of beeves, with about three thousand head to a herd.

We were traveling on the Tom Chism Trail, which led to Smoky River. This was in the early days, before there were any railroads to amount to anything in Texas, and cattle had to be driven all the way to Kansas across country.

The Tom Chism Trail was always lined all the way from Texas to Kansas. It was a great sight to see so many cattle driven on this trail, all bound for the same market. One could look forward or backward and not be able to see the end of the long string of cattle.

I was just a young man then, and went along to help drive this herd of cattle to market. I enjoyed the trip very much, as the scenery was beautiful and camping out was delightful for us cowboys.

The grass all along the route was as fine as it could be, and kept the cattle reasonably fat, considering the long journey, and when they reached their destination it would only take a few days rest to get them in perfect condition.

Those were great days in Texas, when money

was plentiful and wages good. We received splendid pay for driving cattle and the work was most enjoyable. Game was plentiful all the way from Texas to Kansas. The country was full of elk, buffalo, antelope and deer, and we always had plenty of venison to eat, after our appetites were sharpened from a day's riding in the saddle.

We had our cattle bedded near the Canadian River one rainy night, and Tom Murphy, of Austin, and I were guarding them. At twelve o'clock that night about fifteen Indians made a sudden raid on the cattle and stampeded them. The cattle and horses were very much frightened and scattered in every direction. All the cowboys came to our rescue.

The first dash the Indians made they cut off about seventy-five cattle from the herd. The other cattle then ran about two miles and a half in a circle before they "broke the mill."

I was on my saddle when the Indians made the raid, but I was nodding. My horse, however, instantly realized the situation and made a spring forward, throwing me behind the saddle before I roused myself sufficiently to know what the trouble was. It happened, however, that I succeeded in grabbing the horn of my saddle, and I finally managed to regain my proper position.

It was impossible to control the cattle, as the Indians had so badly frightened them. All of them got away from us that night except fifty head, and it took us two weeks to gather them all up, as they scattered for miles over the country. When we got them rounded up we took them on to Kansas without further trouble and sold them.

The Indians captured in their raid on our herd about one hundred head of cattle in all, and I imagine they had quite a feast.

IV

A THIEF

While I was in Quanah, in 1896, helping to hold court in the George Isaacs case, four hundred beef steers were brought into town one day from the Spur ranch. Eighteen cowboys came in with the cattle, and before they left town one of them stole a suit of clothes and a gold watch from a Mr. Greathouse, a merchant of Quanah. Bob Dawson came to me while I was in court helping to guard Isaacs and told me that he wanted me to assist them in running down the thief. I told him that I would; so we got our horses and started out after the cowboys.

We followed them fifteen miles to a place where they had stopped for dinner, and we arrested them and told them that we wanted to search the whole outfit for the clothes and watch.

They said, "all right," and we made the search and found the stolen articles; so we took the boss out and told him that he had better advise the guilty party to "own up," or we would have to take the whole bunch back to town. He failed to get a confession from any of them, so we arrested the whole bunch, boss and all, and escorted them to Quanah.

In the party there was one man, who weighed about 260 pounds, who kept edging around me, trying to get hold of my sixshooter, but I stood him off, and we made him hitch up the wagon and take the others back to Quanah. They had a hundred head of cow ponies, and they took them back with them. When we marched into Quanah with the men and ponies, everybody yelled out, "Yonder comes Coxey's army."

About dark one of the men, by the name of Sloane, plead guilty. His brother had begged him to confess, which he did. He was lodged in the Quanah jail, and was charged with stealing enough property to land him in the penitentiary, but the state made it a finable offense, and his companions paid it out and they left together for their ranch, a happy set of cowboys.

PART OF THE RANGER FORCE DETAILED FOR SERVICE AT EL PASO, TEXAS, TO PREVENT THE MAYER-FITZSIMMONS FIGHT.

1, Adj. Genl. W. H. Mabry; 2, Capt. Jno. R. Hughes; 3, Capt. J. A. Brooks; 4, Capt. W. J. McDonald; 5, Capt. J. H. Rogers; 7, John Hess; 8, Bob Chew; 9, —. Throckmorton; 10, J. H. Evetts; 11, George Horton; 12, Billy McCauley; 13, Lee Queen; 14, Wolley Bell; 15, Ed Flint; 17, Ed Donley; 18, W. J. L. Sullivan; 19, Jack Harvell; 20, Bob McClure; 21, Ed Conley; 22, Andy Ferguson; 23, W. M. Burwell; 24, John Moore; 25, C. F. Hiers; 27, T. T. Cook; 28, C. L. Rogers; 29, Doc Neal; 30, Edgar Neal; 31, Ed Bryan; 32, Doctor Lozier; 33, —. Tucker. Those omitted are men whose names are not remembered by the author.

V

BEN HUGHES

While trying to capture Ben Hughes, who was wanted for train robbery in the Indian Territory, the officers had a fierce battle with him, during which Deputy Sheriff Whitehead, who was a Cherokee Indian, was killed. Hughes was tried for this, but was acquitted, as the killing occurred at night and no one saw him shoot Whitehead, and it could not be proven that he was responsible for the officer's death.

I carried Ben Hughes' wife from the Union depot in Fort Worth to the Windsor Hotel, with instructions from Grude Britton, who was sergeant at that time, to make a thorough search for money. Mrs. Windsor, the proprietress of the hotel, assisted me in making the search on Mrs. Hughes' person for the money which we thought her husband had gotten and turned over to her. I got Mrs. Windsor to help me in searching the woman, because I felt a delicacy in making a search on the person of a lady. I had the respect for her that any gentleman should have for a lady, even if I was searching her for stolen money. I only found about twelve or fifteen dollars on her, and she said that was her own money; so I let her keep it. Mrs. Hughes looked to be about twenty-five years of age.

Sam Farmer and Sergeant J. M. Britton took Hughes to Dallas and placed him in jail, and Mrs. Hughes left that evening for Palo Pinto County.

VI

A BUFFALO HUNT

E. N. Waldrup, Bob Gunn and I left Logan's Gap, Comanche County, February, 1877, for Tom Green County on a big buffalo hunt, intending to make Jim Criner's ranch our headquarters. Criner was a brother-in-law of Bob Gunn.

After reaching Tom Green County, I saw about a mile ahead of me a bunch of buffalo, and remarked to one of the boys that I was going to rope one of them. I dismounted, tightened my saddle girths, and mounted again and made for the bunch of buffalo. They were traveling east. The morning was very cold, as the wind was blowing from the east. As soon as they discovered me they started in a run for their life. There were about one hundred and fifty in the bunch. I ran on to a three-year old bull, threw my lariat, but it failed to catch, as I was throwing against the wind, which was very high. The second throw I put him into my loop. The high, fast bucking and pulling came off then and there. Birch, my horse, was not thoroughly trained and didn't like the scent of buffalo at all. I had a hard time controlling him with this raging, rearing beast tied to the horn of my saddle, as this was about the first bunch of buffalo Birch had ever seen, and the only one he had ever been tied to. Birch and I were like the man that bought the elephant—didn't hardly know what to do with him. I made two runs around the buffalo and got his legs tangled in my lariat. I then made a straight run on him, "busting" him against the ground. When he got up he discovered our horses and wagons and took the outfit for his brother bunch of buffalo. He then made a run for horses and wagon, and when we got to the wagon I decided to take him to Jim Criner's ranch, which was about ten or twelve miles distant, and neck him to a steer. I tied him to the hind axle of the wagon, and he led as docile as any horse for about three hundred yards, and all at once he took a notion to stop, and the horses pulling the wagon took a notion to stop also. We started the horses up again, and they kept pulling until they led him over, at the same time jerking his right shoulder out of place. I had him to kill then, and lost my buffalo. This was a grand old hunt, and proved very profitable to us. The buffalo in that country were as thick as cattle and went from three to ten thousand in a bunch. There were also thousands of antelope, and wild turkeys were so thick that they would hardly get out of one's way.

VII

A STOLEN HERD

I was employed, in 1877, by Bill Yoakum, a cattleman, to help him drive a herd of three hundred cattle from his place in Comanche County to Clear Fork, on the Brazos River. While in his service, Yoakum told me that he and Jim Gregg, who was Yoakum's partner for several years, had stolen these cattle and burnt their brands out and put on another brand. He told me that he had stolen the cattle out of Tarrant, Johnson, Collins and other counties, and that he never took over five head out of the same range. He also said that he had made it a rule to steal only from men who were no able to prosecute him heavily if he was caught.

One day Yoakum asked me to join him, saying that we would make a fortune stealing cattle, but I told him that I w o u l d let him know about it later on.

Near Yoakum's place lived a Mrs. Holt, a widow, who had bought a milk cow from Yoakum, paying him a good price for it. Yoakum laughingly remarked to me one day that he had stolen the cow which he had sold to Mrs. Holt from her range and that she didn't know the difference.

I said to myself, "You two dirty thieves" (meaning Yoakum and his partner, Gregg), "if I can catch you I certainly will do so." After that I kept my eyes open and watched Yoakum very closely. Whenever I managed to get off to myself, I walked around the herd and took down the brands of these three hundred cattle that had been stolen from different parties throughout the State.

After procuring sufficient evidence to show that they had stolen the cattle, I went to Brackenridge and informed the sheriff of these facts, and he and I went to the office of the justice of the peace, where I swore out warrants for the arrest of Yoakum and Gregg.

The sheriff sent his deputy, Frank Freeman, with me to make the arrest, and we reached the herd late in the evening. Gregg was with the herd, grazing cattle in a mesquite flat, when we found him, and we arrested him first. Turning my head toward the wagon, I saw Mrs. Yoakum standing on the wagon tongue motioning her husband to run, which he did. Freeman and I immediately placed Gregg in the charge of other officers who had come along, and set out in pursuit of Yoakum. Yoakum was riding a fast saddle mule, but was caught by Freeman and I, and we brought him back to where the other men were.

While the deputy sheriff was reading the warrant to Yoakum, the latter, being angered at me, suddenly made a play for his sixshooter to kill me, but I was too quick for him and blocked his game. Several men who watched us arrest Yoakum and Gregg were in sympathy with them, and claimed that Yoakum did not try to draw a gun on me. The deputy sheriff, being busy reading the warrant, did not see Yoakum's movements, so he could not say whether I was right or wrong in attacking Yoakum. Old Man Wilson (W. R.) seemed to be the "worst stuck" on Yoakum, and

I thought for quite a while that I would have him to kill, but he eventually quieted down.

I ate no supper that night, nor breakfast the next morning, and drank nothing but a little water out of a creek. The following morning we started back to Brackenridge, taking our two prisoners to jail. Mrs. Yoakum accompanied us to town.

When we reached the town, Old Man Wilson, the great friend of Yoakum, swore out a warrant for me, charging me with assault upon Yoakum. They wanted to arrange it so that I couldn't be in Brownwood to appear against Yoakum when the trial came off, but Freeman held himself responsible for me, and in that way blocked their game.

We left the next morning for Brownwood. Frank Freeman and I rode along together, and while discussing various subjects to pass away the time we accidently learned that we were distant relatives. That probably accounts for Frank being so nice to me and afterward showing me so many favors.

While we were in Brackenridge, Yoakum and Gregg employed Attorney Webb to defend them. That night, when we reached camp, Yoakum asked the deputy sheriff if he could talk to me and, being told that he could, he took me off a few yards to make me a proposition. He told me that if I would not appear against him he would go to Brownwood and beat that one case and leave the country with his stock.

"I can not afford to do it," I said, "for such characters as you should be in the penitentiary."

He then went back to the wagon, and Freeman

called me off and asked me what Yoakum had told me, and I repeated the proposition that Yoakum had made to me.

"Those men who w e n t o u t to help arrest Yoakum and Gregg are undoubtedly thieves and thugs themselves from the way they worked against you," said Frank, "and it might be best for you not to go back to Brackenridge, for you will be alone up there since no one knows you except me, and those tough characters might kill you. I know them too well," he continued, "and I am satisfied that Yoakum made a break for his gun, but his friends will swear that he didn't, and that will cause lots of trouble." Frank then told me that he being responsible for me, he could manage it for me if I wanted to get loose.

I told him that I thought it best for me to leave and not go back to Brackenridge; so I left that night for my former home.

Yoakum succeeded in beating his case through a "slick" scheme of his attorney. Webb and his clients worked on Mrs. Holt and won her over to their side. Yoakum bought Mrs. Holt's cow back, and Mrs. Holt swore in court that that was not her cow, and the indictments were quashed. I learned afterward that Mrs. Holt went over to Brownwood in the wagon with Mrs. Yoakum, and it nearly made me lose confidence in the fair sex.

In accordance with his promise to me, Frank Freeman advertised the brands of the stolen cattle, and cattlemen came from several parts of the State and claimed their property.

If I had been easily persuaded, as a great many

young, unfortunate boys are, to join those cattle thieves in their theft of cattle, I would, most likely, have been found later hanging at the end of a rope, or serving a long sentence in the penitentiary.

VIII

THE HANGING OF BILL LONGLY.

On the 11th of October, 1879, I witnessed the execution of Bill Longly, who was hung at Giddings, Lee County, for the murder of Wilson Anderson. The sheriff, Jim Brown, who had charge of the execution, was the noted horse-racer who was afterward killed in Chicago by a policeman.

A little while before the execution the sheriff read the death sentence to Bill, and, pointing to his two hundred guards, he told the people that he had worked three months selecting his men for the occasion, and that he thought he had about the best there was in the country to assist him in the execution. He then asked Bill if he wanted to make a talk. Bill said he did, and pulled his hat off and placed it in a chair. Then, looking calmly over the crowd, he addressed the guards and spectators as follows:

"This is a big crowd to witness the last of me. I know I am surrounded by enemies, but I forgive them for all that they have done against me, and I want them, as well as my friends, to pray for me." Then, continuing, he said, "I understand that my brother, Jim, was in here to kill the man who cuts the rope to hang me. If you are in this crowd, Jim, don't kill anybody on my account. I knew that if I was ever caught I would have to pay the penalty which I am now paying. I hate to die, but I have killed many a man who hated to die as bad as I do now, so I know I am getting my just deserts."

When Bill finished his harangue he knelt between two priests. He had been confined in the jail at Galveston for eighteen months, and while there he had become a Catholic. Each priest put his hand on the man's head, and they knelt together in prayer for several minutes. When he arose he walked straight to the trap-door and, bowing to the crowd, said:

"Good-bye to everybody."

The sheriff immediately placed the cap over his head, the rope around his neck, and bound his hands and feet. Then he got the hatchet and cut the rope. The trap-door swung back, Bill fell through, and his neck was broken.

Mrs. Anderson, the widow of the man whom Longly had murdered, was present at the execution with her two children. When the doctors pronounced Bill to be dead, she remarked that she was satisfied.

Then they let him down and placed him in his coffin. The rope was coiled and laid on his breast, and the lid of his coffin screwed securely on. A sorrowful father then took charge of the remains of his former wayward son.

Bill's cousins had given him a nice suit, and he was neatly dressed. Young and fine-looking, with dark hair and long black mustache, and with a complexion as fair as a lady's, he looked so handsome before his death that it seemed a pity for him to die in such a terrible and unnatural manner.

IX

THE CAPTURE OF HENRY CAROTHERS.

In 1879, John Presall, a Pinkerton detective, told me that he had traced Henry Carothers to the San Bernard River, and that he wanted me and several others to help capture him. Carothers is the man who killed a Mr. Kirk, a prominent man of McDade.

With Willis McMaron and Albert Rosenberg, I immediately left Burton, on my way to join Presall. We traveled all Saturday night and reached the San Bernard River at daybreak on Sunday morning. There we met Presall, who had summoned us, and Sheriff Lewis, of Austin County, Charley Langhammer, John Collar, Bob Flack, Fritz Rosenberg and John Rankin. We all started out immediately in search of Henry Carothers.

Presall had learned that he was hunting on the San Bernard River. Late that evening we learned from two Swede boys where Carother's camp was located. We immediately struck out for the place, but when we reached the camp we found no one in it, although we saw signs which indicated that some parties had left only a little while before.

We lit on their trail and loped our horses nine miles through a country full of nothing but post oaks and rocks. About half a mile from the little town of New Ulm, John Presall said that he and Sheriff Lewis and Charley Langhammer would go ahead, and for us six men to stay about a quarter of a mile in the rear.

A little while after the three men left us we saw, about a quarter of a mile down the road, a wagon with some men in it. Willis McMaron and I had ridden about two hundred yards ahead of the other four, much to their chagrin, and when Presall, Lewis and Langhammer passed the wagon they discovered that Henry Carothers and his father and two others were in it. When they passed them, the officers heard old man Carothers say, in a low tone to his son, "Henry, you know what you have always said." The officers then looked back and, seeing Henry Carothers and his father reaching for their guns, quickly dropped off their horses.

Henry Carothers leaped out with his Winchester and stationed himself behind the rear part of the wagon. His father took a shotgun and jumped over into a field to get behind a fence. When McMaron and I saw these movements, we knew that that was Henry Carothers and his father, so we laid steel to our horses and rode quickly to the rescue of the three officers in front of us.

Two of the men whom we had left behind, John Collar and John Rankin, tore down the fence and rode into the field where old man Carothers had stationed himself. When the old man saw us surrounding them he called out to his son to fire on the front men.

Tom Gentry, a friend of the two Carothers, and a yellow negro, whose name was Guish, were in the wagon. Guish had always promised "Marse Henry" that if the officers ever attacked them he would certainly stay and fight until he was killed. When Henry and his father showed fight Guish at once left the wagon as if he had wings. He jumped over the fence into the field, and for a mile and a half he could not be seen for cotton flying thick around him as he was leaving "Marse Henry." This affair happened about six o'clock in the evening, and the negro ran all the way to Burton, a distance of thirty-five miles, reaching his home at four o'clock the next morning.

Tom Gentry crawled through the fence and went to Mr. Carothers and plead with him not to advise his son to fight, saying that neither one of them had any chance for their lives. The old man paid no attention to him, however, but called out again to his son to fire on the front men. "You and I are good for two men apiece," he told Henry, "and it will never do for you to surrender."

Henry then laid his Winchester down and picked up Gentry's shotgun, and told Gentry that he was going to "initiate" his gun by using it first. Gentry then told Henry, "for God's sake do not fight when you have no chance on earth to win."

Henry then recognized Charley Langhammer, the officer in front who used to be sheriff of Austin County, and who tried hard to capture him when he first committed the terrible murder. Henry had always "had it in" for Charley, so he invited him to come out from behind his horse and they would take a few shots at each other. Charley started out, but Sheriff Lewis called him back and told Henry that if he challenged anyone else to fight him he would order his men to fire on him immediately.

Henry then asked Lewis how many men he had with him.

Lewis replied that he had nine and they were all officers.

He then asked Lewis if any of the Bells were along.

Lewis answered that they were not.

The Bells were kin to Kirk, the murdered man, and Henry dreaded them.

Lewis then told him that if he surrendered the officers would protect him and that he would not be hurt.

Finally, Henry turned to his father and said, "I have a wife and two children, and you have a wife and six children to live for and if we both get killed in this fight they will be left without protection, so if you will keep out of this fight and let me make it myself I will not give up, but if you don't let me fight it out myself I will surrender."

The old man would not consent to surrender, and said that he wanted to fight it out, whereupon Henry laid his Winchester down, climbed into the wagon, and standing on the seat, said:

"Gentlemen, I have surrendered."

We had a bench warrant for him from the governor, so we handcuffed him and shackled him on his horse, which we had procured at New Elm.

Bob Flack and John Rankin took turns about leading the horse on which the prisoner was mounted, but Henry cursed and abused them so, that they tried to shove the job off on me, but I didn't take it, as I didn't relish being abused any more than they did. I told Henry it wouldn't help his case a bit for him to abuse the officers, but it seemed to afford him pleasure and consolation, and he kept on cursing everybody around him.

He told Bob Flack he would give him a thousand dollars if he would arrange it so he could make his escape.

Bob refused the offer, of course, and Henry asked him how many men it would require to take him away from the officers.

Bob told him that he could no be taken; that they would all die before they would give him up.

Henry then informed us that if his brother-in-law, John Williams, happened to find out that he was captured, that he would gather a band of men and take him from the officers and set him free.

At midnight, as we were entering a long lane, we heard a signal at our left on the prairie, and Henry said that that must be Williams and his men.

As soon as we heard the signal, the advance guard saw a light further up the lane. I was then leading Henry's horse, and Presall, the detective, who was at my side, gave me instructions to shoot Henry and cut his horse's rope from my saddle if Williams' men should try to take him away from us. Presall then said that we would all try to win the fight if we were to have an encounter with Williams and his men; so all of us prepared ourselves for any emergency that might occur.

Turning to Henry, I said, "If this is Williams and his bunch, it will go awful hard with you."

I think Henry heard Presall's instructions, for he seemed rather frightened, and, believing strongly that it was Williams and his men up the lane, he called out to Williams, but received no answer.

We held up, and sent the advance guard forward to see who those men were whom we had heard. They came back in a little while and reported that they were a band of cattlemen, and that the signal which we heard to our left came from the cowboys at the herd.

We then resumed our journey, and when we passed these supposed "cattlemen" they lined up on the right side of the lane and held their six-shooters and Winchesters ready for action. I am satisfied that they were a bunch of thieves expecting to be taken by the officers, or they would not have been so well prepared to fight as they were.

We reached Round Top at daybreak, and placed Henry in the calaboose and put two men to guarding him. Then we slept until breakfast at John Rankin's house.

When we put Henry in the calaboose we shackled him securely, as we knew he would make his escape if he had half a chance, for he was in a desperate mood and was a shrewd and daring man. The shackles, which we put on him, were fastened underneath the floor to a sleeper and were not movable. He filled the keyholes of his shackles with small shot, in order to give us all the trouble he possibly could, and when we transferred him, we were detained a long time getting the shot out of the keyholes.

We took him to La Grange. He was tried later on at Bastrop and given a sentence of life imprisonment in the penitentiary, but was pardoned out by the governor after he had served six years of his term. I met him after he was given his freedom, and he was very friendly with me, and, as he was making a splendid citizen, I welcomed his friendship, and told him I was glad to see him a free man and doing well.

"CHEROKEE BILL"
The most noted Outlaw of the Territory.
Hung at Ft. Smith, Ark.

X

AN EXCITING FISTICUFF

Col. R. D. Hunter wrote to Capt. S. A. McMurray of our company, asking him to let me have a leave of absence to go to Thurber to attend to some anarchists and dynamiters, who were giving the officials a lot of trouble at the mine. He said, in his letter to Capt. McMurray, that he would give me a hundred dollars a month to act as an officer for the company and rid the mine of these characters.

The captain showed me the letter and asked me if I thought I could do the work. I told him that I was perfectly confident that I could. He then asked me if I wanted to go and try it, and I told him that that hundred dollars looked mighty good to me. He gave me permission to go, and I left on the next train for Thurber, and reached there as quickly as possible and made a contract with Hunter to do the work which he had mapped out for me. I remained in the employ of the coal company eight months.

One night, about twelve o'clock, I located thirteen anarchists in one bunch, hidden in a little dark corner, planning to dynamite the mine the following night. I had two men with me, and we crawled up close enough to hear every word that these anarchists said. When they had perfected their plans and stopped their discussion, we arrested the whole bunch and jailed them.

A saloon was run at the mines by Tom Lawson,

who had a ten-year lease on the building. Lawson also owned a fourth interest in the mine, but he and Col. Hunter, the president, had a falling out for some cause, and Lawson got to standing in with the tough element.

One night I heard a pistol shot in the saloon and ran in there to investigate, believing that somebody had been killed. When I reached the inside, I learned that Lawson, who was behind the bar drunk, had shot at a miner, but failed to hit him. This was on pay night and everybody was full of beer and whiskey, and I had already filled the calaboose with drunken men.

I decided to arrest Lawson and put him in with the other men, but when I advanced on him he made a play for his sixshooter, but I fell squarely on top of him with my gun, removing enough skin from his head to half-sole a number 10 shoe. He swore that he would not be locked up, but I put him in the calaboose, all the same, and he was made to pay his fine as any other man.

After paying his fine, Lawson left immediately to report me to Capt. McMurray. Col. Hunter saw Lawson in Fort Worth looking for McMurray and wired me about it, saying that he (Hunter) would stand between me and all danger.

About two weeks after that Capt. McMurray came to Thurber and told me that he understood that I had knocked Lawson in the head, and that he wanted to know the cause of it.

I told him that Lawson was disturbing the peace and that he had shot at a miner, and when I tried to arrest him he attempted to draw a gun on me, and that I hit him with my sixshooter instead of shooting him with it. "I disarmed him and put him in jail," I continued, and my captain replied that I ought to have broken his neck.

About two months after that, Lawson and his bartender, Malcom, and Col. Hunter, all three met in a drug store. Hunter and Lawson began cursing each other, and I heard the row and rushed into the store just in time to see Hunter burst the bottom of a spittoon out over Tom Lawson's head. Hunter then threw a box of cigars at him, striking Lawson in the ear and scattering cigars all over the floor. I noticed Malcom slipping up behind Col. Hunter, preparing to hit him in the back of the head. Just as he started to strike Hunter, however, I struck Malcom myself, in time to stop what would have been a dreadful blow. Malcom whirled around and saw that it was I who hit him. I struck him five times in the face, but he did nothing but back off the gallery. I struck him once again when he reached the outside and kicked him off the gallery. I thought I had him whipped, but when he got up he said he would fight me if I would pull my sixshooter off. He was a stout man and weighed about 230 pounds, but I was not afraid of him. I removed my sixshooter and threw it over to Henry Kronk, the druggist, and told him to look out for it. I then pitched into Malcom again, striking him in the face. He suddenly threw his big arm around my neck and pressed my head aganist his body. I could not get my head free without breaking my neck, and, having the advantage of me in that respect, he commenced beating my head, nose and eyes until my face looked like jelly. I do not know what would have become of my face if Bob Ward, the company's lawyer, had not come to my rescue. Ward knocked Malcom loose from me and knocked him twelve feet from where we were clinched. Tom Lawson then knocked Ward down, he falling on top of Malcom. Hunter was pacing around after Lawson with a heavy rock, but never did get in his lick.

When a carpenter, who was working near by, saw the dangerous position that I was in when Malcom had me clinched, he ran to my rescue with a hatchet in his hand. He was frightened and as pale as death, and he intended to cut Malcom loose with his hatchet, but Ward got in ahead of him and did the work for him.

My face was in a terrible fix, and the doctor put a beef steak on it to draw the blood out of the bruised places. My face was so badly bruised and swollen that one could hardly tell where my eyes and nose were. I had a girl then, whom I was loving very dearly, and I could not go to see her for a long time, on account of the sad condition of my complexion. I shunned her everywhere for quite a while; for I well knew that it would never do to let "Betty" see me in that fix.

I went to the justice of peace the next morning after the fight and paid my fine, which amounted to twelve dollars. The money was paid back to me by Col. Hunter. Hunter, Ward, Malcom and Lawson all fought their cases hard, but it cost them about two hundred dollars apiece before they were through, while the fight only cost me twelve dollars, and the money was refunded to me.

XI

WATERSPOUT AT QUANAH

On the fourth day of June, 1891, one of the hardest rains that I ever experienced began falling in Quanah at noon, and lasted all the afternoon and throughout that night. I knew that the rain was going to do lots of damage if it kept up, so I resolved to go down to the railroad bridge before the north-bound passenger train arrived to see if the dam was in good condition.

I held my watch in my hand, and when it was nearly time for the train to arrive I walked down to the bridge, where the passenger was to cross. I stood near the railroad tank until the train came in, but it was raining so hard that I could not see the smoke from the engine as the train came down the track.

The passenger arrived on time, and stopped on the east side of the tank to take water, while I was on the west side examining the dam. I soon saw that the dam was giving away, so I waded into the tank and attracted the attention of the engineer. He could not hear what I was saying, so he left his engine and waded in the tank close enough to me to understand what I had to say. I told him that the dam was breaking, but he did not see any signs of it from where he was, and, thinking that I was unduly excited, he decided that I was mistaken, and, going back to his engine, he reversed the throttle and prepared to cross the bridge. About that time the dam broke and was swiftly washed away to the other side. The engineer stopped his engine just in time to save the train from going across the dam and being thrown overboard. Nearly four hundred passengers, including many women and children, were on the train, and they seemed to be very grateful to me for the part that I played in saving their lives. The train crew were also thankful that they did not get any further than they did before the accident occurred.

When the dam broke, the railroad bridges, the county bridge, two or three houses, and a number of windmills were all washed away. Several other rivers in that part of the state got on a rampage, and quite a number of county and railroad bridges, besides those around Quanah, were destroyed.

XII

FIVE PEOPLE BEG FOR FOOD

While doing duty as a policeman in the State Capitol building in Austin, in 1903, I boarded at the Capitol Hotel.

One cold, rainy day I left the table, after eating my dinner, and discovered two ladies and three children standing at the screen door on the outside. I asked them what they wanted, and they said they had sent a little boy in there with a note asking for money enough to get dinner for all five of them. They said they were "awful hungry."

The little boy came out in a minute, and said he had seen all those men in the dining room, but they would not give him a cent. The little fellow, who was about four years of age, had tears in his eyes and looked as if he was sentenced to his death. A baby boy had gone into the dining room, filled with men drawing their five dollars a day, and hadn't procured enough money to feed himself.

His mother and the elder lady, who was about sixty-five years of age, said, "I guess we'll have to go, but we are awful hungry."

I told them to sit down in the sitting room; that I was going to see that they got something to eat. I saw the proprietor and got him to prepare a table for the five people. I then carried the poor people into the dining room and seated them around the table.

I went to the waiters and told them to give those people something of everything they had and plenty of it. The waiters carefully and courteously attended to their wants, and the ladies and the children ate to their hearts' content. I never felt happier in my life than I did when I watched them enjoy that meal. When they got through eating, they asked me if it would be any harm for them to carry the scraps away for their supper.

I told them that it was no harm at all, and I went to work at once and rustled up the biggest paper sack in the house for them, and told them to take everything they could find, which they did.

After dinner they went into the sitting room and sat around the stove to warm themselves and rest, as they were quite weary. They thanked me over and over for what I had done for them, and the old lady asked God to bless me for what she called "my act of kindness," and asked Him to bless all my efforts in life.

The boys were too small to know what all this meant, and they sat on the floor, their hunger appeased, and laughed and played. This was a sad sight to me, and when the women began crying I could not keep the tears from my own eyes.

These unfortunate people were from the country, and boll weevils and other things had destroyed their crops for two years and left them destitute. They were in such a pitiful plight that I was thankful that I was able to aid them, and that $1.25 that I gave for their dinner did me more good and furnished me more happiness than any other sum of money I ever spent.

XIII

THE MURDER OF HARTMAN

I was ordered by the governor in 1890 to go to San Saba, as District Court was to convene there and the presence of Texas rangers in that town was greatly needed; for the people of that district were divided into two opposing factions, and the bitterness that existed between them had become intense.

Since 1880 San Saba had been the center of a disturbance, caused by the organization of a "mob," whose operations extended into several other counties in that district.

In other words, a number of people had banded together to protect themselves against the depredations of cattle thieves and other criminals, who were numerous in that part of the state. A number of people lived in that district who had no regard for law and order, and stole so many cattle, horses and hogs that the people became aroused, and decided to take the law into their own hands and punish the guilty parties as they saw fit, and for this reason the club, afterward referred to as "the mob," was organized.

The lawless element, of course, arrayed themselves against the mob faction. Many good people also lined up against it, as they did no believe in mob spirit and thought the law should be allowed to take its course. Thus a strong organization, called the "anti-mob," grew into activity and bitterly opposed the other faction.

The mob faction, however, was the stronger of the two sides in numbers and influence, and in San Saba County, their greatest stronghold, they elected one of their men sheriff.

The mob did some good work for a while, but, like all organizations of that character, it finally went too far, and became more oppressive as it grew in power. Quite a number of bad citizens were "slick" enough to slip over to the stronger faction—the mob element—and, as they did so, they played a big part in changing the purpose and power of that organization from good to bad.

When the mob was first organized it began to put down lawlessness, but in 1890, ten years later, the bitter feeling that existed between the mob and anti-mob factions had reached such a high pitch that there was much fighting and disorder. Lawlessness was encouraged by both sides and could not be prevented by local authorities. Killings became rather frequent occurrences, and thieves took advantage of the numerous opportunities and stole live stock without fear of prosecution.

Thus the criminal docket was full of important cases, but the prosecuting attorney could not go about his work unless he was given protection by the State; so the governor sent me, as I have stated before, to San Saba to help them hold court.

Red Murphy and Tom Platt, also rangers, were with me, and we arrived at San Saba on the following Sunday about noon. After eating dinner at the hotel, we walked up the street and found the town full of men, as court was to convene the next morning.

The men were sitting or standing around in

groups of twelve or fifteen, and were discussing with some fervor the convening of court. They had come to town to see that things were run to suit them when court opened, and they meant "business," for the stores were full of their guns and ammunition which they had brought with them.

While passing one group, we heard a man inquire who we were, and another man replied that we were Texas rangers; whereupon they all laughed, some of them remarking that if we ever got three miles out of town we would never live to get back. We heard the remark, but paid no attention to it.

On the following Tuesday night some one came to the hotel where we were staying and asked the proprietor, Jim Darfmyer, if the Texas rangers were not staying with him. Darfmyer told them that we were, and the visitor asked him to call us, which he did.

When we got downstairs we met Nat Hartman, whose home was on the Colorado River. He seemed very anxious about something and informed us that his brother, Edd Hartman, was missing, and that he feared he had been killed. The Hartmans were members of the anti-mob faction, and Nat Hartman told us that this was the first time in nine years that his brother had been outside of his house after sundown.

We told him that we would go by and get Sheriff Howard and commence looking for his brother. Nat objected to us getting Howard. We told him that we would have to have the sheriff with us, so we went by and called for Howard, who joined us in the search.

We reached the home of Nat Hartman's father a little before day, and just before sunrise we left Hartman's house and started down the river, the way they claimed Edd went off the day before at one o'clock. We walked about three-quarters of a mile, and found the dead body of the man for whom we were searching, lying in the bed of the river.

We traced two men's tracks from the body to a house, sixty steps away, where a Mr. Campbell, one of Howard's deputy sheriffs, lived.

Campbell was out in the yard when he saw us coming, but he started in a fast walk to the house when he discovered us. We stopped him before he got very far, but he said something to his wife, who was standing in the doorway, and she whirled back into the building, returning in a second or two with something in her hand, which she held under her apron.

We were satisfied that she had his sixshooter, and we ordered her not to go near her husband. She then went back into the house. We arrested Campbell and his two sons, Meck and Dave, and five other men in his neighborhood. We reached San Saba with them a little after dark that evening, and locked them up in a little house that Darfmyer let us have for that night. We did not let them sleep together and kept them from talking with each other, so they would not "make medicine."

About an hour or two before day, Campbell asked me to let him get up and sit by the stove.

I told him that would be alright, and he came over and began talking to me. He ran his hand over his face and said his face was paining him. He also claimed that his mule pitched him off a day or two before that, and threw him into a rough place, bruising his face up badly. He said he couldn't understand what was the matter with his mule; that he used to be a good mule, but had acted mighty strangely of late. He then claimed that the mule had also thrown one of his boys recently and bruised his face up considerably.

The next morning we had all eight of the men up before the grand jury. Campbell testified before the grand jury that a little grey mare had fallen down with him in a rough place and bruised his face. Another man before the grand jury testified that a dun mare had fallen down with Campbell twelve miles further up the river. They made such conflicting statements in trying to get out of trouble that the grand jury indicted Dave Campbell and his father for the murder of Edd Hartman.

Dave Campbell jumped his bond and was caught seven years later in Arizona, where he was living under the name of "Alex Miller," and was brought back to San Saba, but he was acquitted.

Old man Campbell got a change of venue to Fort Mason, and was convicted and sentenced to seven and a half years in the penitentiary, but appealed his case. He was tried sixteen times in eight years, and finally got off on a light sentence of two and a half years, and went to the penitentiary from Lampasas to serve it out. I had to go to court twice a year for eight years to testify in that case.

Mr. Hartman, the father of the murdered man, is now dead, but he lived to fight the case for eight long years, and finally heard the sentence read to Campbell. In fighting the case he spent every dollar he had, and sold his farm and home and stock, in order to keep up the prosecution, and when he died at the age of seventy-seven years he was renting land. He had remained faithful to his son to the last.

XIV

THE CHASE AFTER DEL DEAN, WHEN I BREAK MY ARM AND ANKLE

While court was in session at San Saba, Del Dean, an alleged horsethief, was notified that he had been indicted by the grand jury for stealing live stock. Dean at once mounted his horse and left town. Sheriff Hawkins asked me to capture Dean, saying that Dean had just left town, going out on the Llano road.

I mounted my horse and started out in pursuit. Riding fast, I soon came in sight of Dean, who was urging his horse to the utmost speed. I clamped spurs to my horse and commenced to gain still more on Dean, and for some time we kept up a hot race.

It was misting snow and the weather was raw and cold. I was going down hill as fast as my horse could run, when he suddenly struck a flat table rock and let his feet slip from under him. He fell, and I was thrown twenty-three feet from the saddle. My horse was running so fast when he fell that it was remarkable that I was not killed. When my horse and I took that sudden stop, I fell into a pile of rocks, and my head was badly bruised, my face terribly lacerated, my right arm broken, and my ankle sprained.

Dean, of course, made his escape, and I do not think that he saw my horse fall with me. I was badly crippled up, and was treated by Doctors George and John Sanderson (brothers) for forty-six days. It was two years before I had any strength in my right hand and arm. I learned to shoot left-handed, and when my right arm got strong again, I could shoot as well with one hand as I could the other.

Dean was captured by Edgar T. Neal after the latter became sheriff of San Saba County. When I went back to San Saba I went to the jail and saw Dean. All the prisoners shook hands with me except Dean. He had turned out his beard and I could not place him; so I asked him his name.

He said, "I am Del Dean, the man whom you were pursuing when you broke your arm, and for that reason I thought probably you would not want to speak to me."

I assured him that he was mistaken; that I had no ill feeling toward him at all. I told him that while it was my duty to pursue him, it was natural for him to try to escape, and that I did not blame him with the accident. I told him that I felt sorry for him because he was in jail and hoped he would lead a better life when he got free again.

"Captain Brooks of Company A, and his seven Rangers."

XV

The Capture and Escape of Morris, the Noted Murderer

In 1891 there lived in the little town of Vernon, one Jim Morris, and the two Moss brothers, who left together, during that year, for Greer County, where the three men were to take up land. The two Moss brothers had between them about five or six hundred dollars, which fact was known to Morris when the three left Vernon together. After reaching Salt Fork, which is in Greer County, they pitched camp to rest up a bit. While there, Morris and one of the Moss boys walked out a mile or so from the wagon to kill some game. After being gone a little while, Morris suddenly turned his gun on Moss and fired, killing him instantly. After burying the dead body in a sandhill, he went back to camp and told the other Moss boy that his brother had sent back for him and the wagon, as he had found a much better place to camp, and for him to hitch up and bring everything to the new stopping place. There happened to be two cow-punchers at the camp at this time who heard the conversation. Moss was sick, and when the two left, as Moss supposed, for the new camping place, he lay down in the bottom of the wagon, with his head near Morris, who was driving.

Ignorant of the terrible fate that had just overtaken his brother a little while before, Moss unsuspectingly put his hat over his face so he could rest easier, with the sun's rays thus kept from his eyes.

Morris took advantage of this opportunity, and shot and killed the sick man, the bullet passing through his hat and blowing his brains out. He then threw the body out of the wagon and buried it in a nearby sandhill, exactly as he had disposed of the remains of the other man. Besides getting all of their money, he kept one of their watches, and also the coat which he took from his first victim. This coat had a bullet hole through the back, indicating the manner in which the man had been slain. Among other things found in the coat was a note which Moss had written to a young lady asking her for her company to church. The lady had accepted his invitation, according to this note, which had slipped into the lining through a worn-out pocket. When this murder occurred I was stationed in Quanah.

At that time there was no jail at Mangum, where we caught Morris, so we placed the prisoner in the calaboose, but as there was strong talk of lynching him, the officers removed him to Quanah, where he was safely landed in the county jail. He was kept there about two years, and was closely guarded a greater part of that time by some of the rangers. He was tried on two indictments for murder and was sentenced to hang in both cases.

He appealed his case, however, and got a new trial, but the jury again brought in a verdict of death. He became very desperate, and was a hard man to keep imprisoned. One night during his trial, while being guarded by Bob Dawson, a constable of that county, he picked his shackles with a writing pen and broke away. In escaping he jumped from a two-story window, and was at large three days and nights before he was recaptured and placed in jail. Morris kept us mighty busy before he was found, and, when we did get him, we took him in a few days to Fort Worth for safe keeping, until the day of his execution; but he succeeded in breaking away from that place, also, and never has been captured nor located since. At the time of his escape Morris was twenty-seven years of age, tall, broad-shouldered, and very handsome.

One morning at sunrise, while in the brakes searching for Morris, we looked up the draw which led into Pease River and saw a fire. Thinking we would find our game, we at once surrounded the place where we saw the fire and smoke, but found instead an escaped convict. With him was a woman dressed in man's clothes. Her hair was cropped short, and on her heels she wore a pair of Petmaker spurs. She also wore a California suit of clothes, a Stetson hat, a shop-made pair of boots, and a blue shirt and necktie. She was a Mistress Jennie Bates, and was stolen away from her home in Palo Pinto County by this convict. We took from her a .45 Colt's sixshooter, a Winchester and a scabbard belt full of cartridges.

The woman, who weighed nearly a hundred and thirty-five pounds, looked to be about twenty-five years of age and a little over five feet tall. With black hair and dark eyes, she appeared to be a good looking man. The couple had stolen four head of horses, so we put them in jail at Quanah. The convict had escaped from the penitentiary after serving five years of a ten-year sentence for horse stealing. He was tried in Quanah for his latest thefts, and sent back to the penitentiary to finish serving his first sentence, with an addition of five years for his last crime. The woman got a change of venue from Quanah to Vernon and came clear. The ladies of Vernon felt sorry for her and dressed her up in woman's clothing. Mrs. Wheeler was the only white woman I ever arrested. Mr. J. M. Britton, a ranger, aided in making the capture.

XVI

THE ARREST OF HOLLINGSWORTH

I received a warrant from Austin, in 1891, to arrest O. N. Hollingsworth. He was then living eighteen miles west of Quanah, and seven miles south of Kirkland. Pick Gipson, the sheriff, and Lon Lewis went with me after Mr. Hollingsworth. Hollingsworth knew Lon Lewis and Sheriff Gipson, but he had never seen me; so, when we got within a half mile of Mr. Hollingsworth's house, they proposed that I go down to the house and see if he was there, saying that if he was they would come on in a short time, and for me to remain until they arrived there. They told me not to try to arrest him, for they were pretty well satisfied, since the old man's case was a bad one, that he would more than likely make a fight. When I rode up to the gate, I called out to the people, it being after dark, and a young man, who looked to be about seventeen years old, came out.

I asked him if he had seen a man pass there riding a grey horse and leading a black, or riding a black and leading a grey. I told him that this man was about six feet two and one-half inches tall, and had red curly hair and a heavy red mustache. I said that I wanted this man in Baylor County for the theft of these two horses. He said that he had not seen the man nor the horses. He asked me then to get down and spend the night with them. I told him that as my horse and I were very badly jaded I would like to stay there that night. I asked him if I would be imposing on the family, and inquired if his father and mother were at home. He said that they were in the house, and I told him that I would stay.

I led my horse up through the gate, and he remarked "Let's go and put your horse up."

I told him that I would have to have a drink of water before I put my horse up; that I was nearly dying with thirst. The water barrel was sitting right in front of the door, and I could see it in the light. He insisted very much on me putting my horse up before I got the water, but I could see the old man standing in the door, and I was satisfied that he would step out in the dark and I would fail to see him that night, as the lot was on the other side, in the rear. I went on up to the front door and spoke to the old gentleman and took a drink of water.

Then I asked the old gentleman if his name was Hollingsworth.

He said it was.

I said, "I have papers for you, Mr. Hollingsworth."

"Where are they from?" he asked.

"From Austin."

"Well, alright," he said.

I turned my horse over to the young man and told him to hitch him. Then I stepped into the building, and the old gentleman and I sat down. Mrs. Hollingsworth was reading a book and never looked up nor spoke to me for twenty minutes, and, when she did, she asked if I had been to supper.

I told her that I had eaten some cheese and crackers that I had with me.

She said, "You had better let me go and fix something for you; I have plenty cooked." I insisted that she not put herself to any trouble, but she went, anyway, and fixed the table. I am satisfied that Mrs. Hollingsworth thought that I would leave her husband in the house while I went to eat. That would have given the old gentleman a chance to make his escape; so, when I started out, I told him to go out ahead of me. This little eating house was about twenty steps from the main building that we were in. I ate supper, and we went back to the dwelling and seated ourselves.

The old gentleman commenced crying and started to the bureau, where there was a double-barrel shotgun and a Winchester, one on each side. He was half way to the bureau, when the thought struck me that he might make a bad play with those guns, being stirred up as he was and crying; so I halted him, and told him to come back and take his seat. He told me that he only wanted to get the hair brush and brush his hair and beard, but I told him that he could do that in the morning.

About that time Gipson and Lewis came up, and I was very glad to see them. I had been looking for them for some time; for they told me that if I did not return they would come to me in a half hour, as they would know that he was at home; but it was all of an hour and a half before they came to me. They put their horses up, and Mrs. Hollingsworth began to fix beds for all of us. This building had only one room. It was cut back in a hill and planked up on each side and in front, making a comfortable house. Mrs. Hollingsworth made us a pallet in the front part of the building. She and her husband slept in the back, and there was a curtain in the center of the house that cut them off from the others. She told me that I could lie down and rest easy; that she would be responsible for her husband; that there was no way for him to escape. I noticed two windows in the back part of the building; so I told Mrs. Hollingsworth that I made it a point to guard all prisoners, and for her and her family to fix and lie down, and I would pull the curtains back so we could guard the old gentleman.

It was seven miles from there to Kirkland, and eighteen miles from Kirkland to Quanah; so we ate breakfast the next morning and got off in time to meet the south-bound train at Kirkland. Mr. Hollingsworth's boy took him in the buggy to Kirkland. When we reached Kirkland, Pick Gipson, the sheriff, took him to Quanah on the train, and Lon Lewis and I rode through horseback.

When Mr. Hollingsworth separated from his wife and two or three little girls, it was such a sad scene to witness, that I never will forget it. His wife clung to his neck, and those sweet little girls held to his arms and legs. I thought I never would get away from the sound of his wife's and children's screams. This was, indeed, a sad morning to me, and the family had my deepest sympathy.

When we reached Quanah, I learned at our camp that Pick Gipson had turned Mr. Hollingsworth over to the rangers, and he remained at our camp three days and nights before we sent him to

Austin. While at camp, eating our grub, I asked the old gentleman one day if he would like to have a hotel dinner. He said he would, so I took him to the Quanah Hotel and gave him a good dinner. He asked me to walk up stairs with him, and he showed me some pictures of Jersey cows and calves, which were hanging on the wall. They were beautiful, and he told me that his grown daughters had drawn them. He cried, and said, "Sullivan, I am no thief. My children overdrew on me. They were 'high livers' and they got me behind with the State. That is the reason you have me arrested." Hollingsworth was then about sixty-five years old, very straight and erect, and fine looking, and was highly educated. I am satisfied that he was no thief, but his children were expensive in their way of living, and caused him to fall behind and make this great mistake with the State. When he got into this trouble he was holding an office in Austin. Before that he taught school and bore a good name. He gave bond in Austin, but jumped it and made his escape. His wife sold her home, and his two daughters sold theirs—a section of land apiece—and paid the bond off. I have never heard of Hollingsworth since.

XVII

THE CAPTURE OF MAYES, THE NOTED HORSE THIEF

While stationed at Quanah, Texas, I was notified one evening by Col. Rush that Dock James, alias Dock Mayes, a noted horse thief, was camping near Quanah, and that he was stealing cattle and horses throughout that part of the country.

Col. Rush had just arrived in Quanah on the train from Colorado City. He told me that he had two herds of cattle, near Quanah, that had been driven in from Colorado City by his hands.

As Mayes was wanted in seven counties, I thought I had better make good work of him; so I took Frank Hofer, a ranger, and Bob Collier, a deputy sheriff, and started after this cattle thief. I at once went north with them to Groesbeck River, about five miles out of town, where I found a herd of cattle. I asked the man who had charge of the cattle if that herd belonged to Col. Rush. He replied that they did not; that Rush's herd was south of the Fort Worth & Denver road; so I bade him good-bye and started south.

When I got to the railroad I met two ladies in a buggy going west, up the track. I looked around, and about five miles south of the track I saw the herd, but I was satisfied that these ladies were going up the track to another herd, and, thinking that the cattle west of us were Rush's, I plead with Bob Collier to go with me, and we would follow the ladies. I was afraid that the ladies would inform

Mayes that the officers were around, and told Bob that that was why I wanted to go up the track then, but Bob was hard-headed and would not go with us; so we turned and ran our horses to the herd that was directly south of us, and made the five miles in a little while.

When I reached the herd I saw a man sitting on a big black horse. I asked him if this was Col. Rush's herd, and he said, "No; Rush's herd is at Quanah at the railroad tank watering."

I knew that was a lie, for I had not been away from Quanah more than three-quarters of an hour, as I had been riding fast all the time.

I rode around the herd and asked one of the hands, a Mexican, if he could tell me where either one of Col. Rush's herds was. In reply, he pointed west, the direction in which the two ladies were going, and said, "Yonder is the herd on that high divide about five miles from here." Then I was somewhat vexed, when I remembered that Bob would not consent to us following the buggy a little while before.

Although our horses were hot and tired, I told Bob and Frank to put theirs beside mine and we would run them over to the other herd. I told Bob that since he had acted such a fool, and caused this trouble, I would make him kill that horse of his; so we laid the steel to our horses and pulled for that other five-mile heat.

We had arrived within three-quarters of a mile from Mayes' camp and the herders had failed to see us, as we were in a flat covered with mesquite timber, and they were at the top of a hill, right on the divide.

The two ladies, whom we had seen going up the track, had reported to them that we were coming. A man, calling himself Jackson, was sent at once to the wagon at their camp to inform Mayes that we were coming, but he did not get to deliver his message. As we were nearing the divide, Jackson ran his horse into us at full speed. I stopped him and asked him where he was going. He replied that he was going to camp to change horses. I told him that his horse didn't seem to be very tired from the way he was moving out. I then put him under arrest and told him to tell me the truth.

"I want a fellow," I said, "by the name of Dock James, alias Dock Mayes, and don't you tell me anything but the truth. Is he with the herd, or is he at camp?"

He replied that he was at the camp.

I asked him how far it was to the camp.

He said it was about a mile and a half.

I then told him to put his horse beside mine and take me the nearest way to camp.

When I got within eight hundred yards of their camp, I saw the same man whom I had met sitting on the black horse at the other herd, five miles away. He was the one who had told me such a story about Bush's cattle being in Quanah, watering at the railroad tank. He, also, had a message to deliver to Mayes about us, and had run his horse fast enough to beat us a minute or two, but too late to give Mayes sufficient time to get away. We saw him rush up to the wagon and tell Mayes that we were coming. Mayes sprang up and, in a stooping position, went in a trot to his saddle, about thirty yards away, and pulled his Winchester out of the scabbard. The man on the black horse immediately put spurs to his steed and left for his herd. When I saw Mayes making for his Winchester I thought I could rush in and get him before he reached it. I had no more use for Jackson, so I told Bob and Frank, both, to follow me and let him go. I then spurred my horse up and went straight for Mayes, with Bob following me. Bob, however, had told Frank to stay behind and guard Jackson, which was not my wish, and Frank did what Bob had requested him to do.

Bob stayed with me about three hundred yards, and then dropped behind, and when I had gotten within two hundred yards of Mayes, I heard him (Bob) yelling at me to hold up. I had gone too far by this time to turn back; so I paid no attention to Bob, but kept jerking "cat hair" out of my horse's sides.

When I had gotten within sixty yards of the wagon, Mayes yelled to me that he would kill me if I crowded him any more. About that time my horse became frightened at some blankets hanging out on a mesquite bush, and commenced jumping a thousand ways a second; but I kept pulling for the wagon. Mayes had gotten behind the wagon, and was at this time sitting by the wheels with his Winchester at his shoulder. When I saw him and remembered his reputation as a fine shot and a dangerous man, I said to myself, "I am a dead man." I jumped my horse over the wagon tongue, which placed me within six feet of Mayes. I sat my horse down, and pointed my gun at Mayes and told him to surrender. He said he would. I ordered him to throw his Winchester on the ground, which he did. I searched him for his sixshooter, and picked his Winchester up. About that time. Bob Collier, the deputy sheriff, came up.

Mayes asked me why I crowded him as I did. "If I had had my Winchester loaded," he said, "you would have been in hell right now. This is the first time in fourteen years that the magazine of my rifle has ever been empty."

I asked him how it came to be empty then.

He replied that one of the boys had gone out to shoot rabbits a little while before that, and emptied the magazine and had forgotten to reload it.

Then I asked him if his name was Mayes, and he replied that it was.

I asked him if "James" would not suit him better; but he only smiled.

I then asked him if he had a horse.

He replied that he had a little old sore-back cow pony.

About that time Frank Hofer came up, bringing Jackson with him. I scolded Frank a little bit about staying with Jackson instead of coming with me as I had requested him to.

I told Jackson to go with Frank and get Mayes' horse, which he did, returning in a few minutes. I found that Mayes had lied. His "little sore-back cow pony" was a thoroughbred racehorse, and as pretty as a peach.

I handcuffed Mayes and took his bridle reins. Then I tied a rope around his animal's neck and wrapped the other end around the horn of my saddle, and let Mayes mount his horse. After we started off Mayes asked me to let him have the reins, as his horse traveled so badly when he did not have reins in his hands. I had a suspicion that he intended to attempt to make his escape, so I did not grant his request.

I put him in the county jail at Quanah. He was wanted at Weatherford for horse theft. He was sentenced to the penitentiary for nine years; was tried again in Colorado City, and sentenced for an additional nine years. He was wanted in five more counties, but did not answer for the other charges. After serving six years of his term of nine years, he was pardoned out of the penitentiary by Gov. Culberson.

XVIII

EXCITING EXPERIENCES WHILE PURSUING BILL JAMES

I went, in 1891, while stationed at Quanah, to institute a search for Bill James, who had foully murdered his brother, John, at Bill's home.

James was supposed to be hiding in the Comanche Strip; so I took George Black, Frank Hofer and Billy McCauley and went to Greer County, where we pitched camp on the North Fork of Red River, about three miles from Navajoe. We rode every day for five months, and scouted the country all around there. Though our main object was to capture James, we arrested a number of criminals and put a stop to some of the lawlessness that occurred on the border.

We had a number of amusing, as well as exciting, experiences while trying to capture James. I told James' brother-in-law one day that I thought James was in Quanah Parker's camp, or in that part of the strip. At that time Quanah Parker's camp was near Fort Sill. The brother-in-law told me that I would be apt to find him there, and I announced that I was going to take all the rangers and go to that part of the strip to look for Bill.

I planned and talked about the trip for several days, to make everybody think that I was really going to Fort Sill after James. My real intention, however, was to allow James' brother-in-law and other friends plenty of time to get word to him that the officers were to be out of the way on a cer-

SERGEANT W. J. L. SULLIVAN IN 1896

tain date, and he could come home and see his two-weeks' old babe, which I thought he would do. Then I was to go out a few miles and drop back suddenly at the right moment and capture James.

An old man, who lived in the community, wanted to go along with us to help about camp, and play the fiddle for us and hunt game. He was a privileged character in the community, and very amusing as well as useful; so I told him he could go with us. He was elated over the thought of going with us and said he would play his fiddle at night, and in the day time he would kill all the birds on Bitter Creek for us to eat.

When the day came for us to leave a number of men came to see us off. We packed our bedding and provisions in the wagon, and the old man got on with his shotgun and fiddle, and we started off in grand style.

We traveled slowly and lost as much time as we could, in order to be as close to his home as was possible under the circumstances when night came on.

At six o'clock in the evening I told the driver to pull out to the left of the road. It was eight miles from any water, and I remarked that we would have "dry camp."

The fiddler and bird man asked me what I meant by "dry camp."

I told him that we were to do without water.

He said that he had been thirsty an hour or two and had been wishing that I would stop and pitch camp, so he could get a drink of water.

I told the old man that we rangers didn't drink

but once a day, and that the mules and horses were trained the same way.

He said if he had known all this at first he wouldn't have come along.

We told him that we were a little thirsty ourselves, but if he would play the fiddle for us it would help us to pass the time away and endure our thirst. The man played and sang for us a little while, and then rolled up in his blankets and was soon asleep, calling hogs and sawing gourds in that good old happy way.

After waiting there several hours, I decided we had been away long enough for James to have had time to reach his home; so I woke the man up and told him that we were going back to the river, where we could get a drink of that good muddy water.

He said that he could not understand our movements; that he thought we were to be gone several days.

I told him that we would have to go, and, turning to the driver and the other boys, I said that we would have to travel quietly. We had good luck in fording the river, but when we reached the other side we found two roads, one leading to the left and and the other to the right. I had to study a moment to determine what we had better do.

I was afraid James had caught on to us; so I sent George Black and Frank Hofer around the left-hand road, and Farris and I went the other way. I thought, by doing that, we would catch James, even if he became suspicious and left the river to go back to his old hiding place.

I told Black and Hofer that if they found the

gates down, they must run fast and that we would do the same thing. The two roads were only half a mile apart, and I could hear a dog barking further up the road on the left, and, thinking it might mean that someone had gone ahead to notify James of our coming, we ran as swiftly as our horses could carry us, all four of us reaching James' house at the same time.

We quickly dismounted, and the other boys surrounded the house while I knocked at the front door.

A lady asked who I was and what I wanted. I told her that I was Sullivan and wanted her husband, Bill.

She said he wasn't there, and that I had been searching her house so much that she was not going to open the door.

I told her I couldn't help that, and, though I was sorry for her, I made her open the door at last.

She said she would not turn on a light. I told her I would attend to that part of it alright, and when I went into the house I pulled a handful of matches from my pocket and lit the whole bunch at once, which made a good light.

The boys outside were eagerly watching the house to see if Bill James would run out. I searched the house thoroughly, but could not find my man, and finally decided that he was not there and gave up the hunt.

I was greatly disappointed at my failure, for I wanted James "awful bad." He sent us a number of messages, saying that we had better look out; that he would knock us out of date. If we had met him, though, we would have done what was right by the gentleman.

I was satisfied, after we failed to find him, that he was further from home than we thought he was, and that he failed to learn that we had left Greer County.

Frank Hofer and I thought once that we had him in a cave. The cave was in the side of a big mountain, and we had to climb about two hundred feet to get to it.

When we first entered the cave, Frank and I could walk side by side, but the further we went the narrower the cave got, and we finally had to walk "single file." The cave was small, but we soon saw that it opened into another one.

It was very dark inside the cave, and we had to feel our way as we went. We came to a place through which we had to go sidewise, and at another place we ran across a spring. We could smell bacon, and knew by that and other signs that men had camped in there, and we were also sure that Bill James was at that moment in the back part of that cave. We came across funny things and heard strange noises, and the further we went, the darker it got.

Finally Frank asked me if I didn't think we were acting foolishly in going blindly into that cave.

"I expect we are," I replied.

"Let's get out," said Frank.

I told him I was willing; so we groped our way out, and we were glad to see daylight again.

It was about thirty feet to the top of the mountain, and we knew the cave must have extended quite a number of feet upward. There was lots of brush and wood on top; so we decided to throw down some of it and pile it in the cave and set fire to it and smoke the man out.

Frank climbed to the top of the mountain and threw the wood down onto a bench that made off from the mountain, and I dragged it back and piled it up in the cave. When we finished our task we ignited the wood and brush and got off a little way to wait for the man to come out.

The wood blazed up in good fashion, but in a little while we commenced wondering where the smoke was going to. We soon found out, however, for the smoke and heat ascended to the top of the mountain inside the cave, but, not being able to get out, it rebounded and began pouring out of the cave in great volume. The heat was intense, and we could not see which way to turn on account of the smoke. Fire gushed out of the cave, and the flames were blown against us, setting us on fire before we could get out of the way. Instead of smoking out men and fighting criminals, we were setting fire to ourselves and fighting the flames.

It would have been better if we had gone on and explored the cave, and let the smoking business alone, but we were afraid to venture too far in when it was so dark, and we did not know what we were going to run into. Somebody told us if we had gone on to the end of the cave, we might have found some money, but I hadn't lost any money in there just at that date, and Frank said he hadn't, so we thought we had no particular amount of business in there, and we decided to beat a retreat.

James was finally captured in the Indian Territory by some United States marshals, and was tried for the murder which he was alleged to have committed, but was acquitted. Before I close this story, however, I shall relate another incident which happened while we were trailing James.

Early one morning the other boys and myself went to the top of a mountain to look down upon James' house through a field glass, and see if we couldn't catch James slipping into his house.

While looking through the glass I discovered a man about two miles from us and a mile from Bill's house. He was walking around another mountain, and held something in his hand that shined so in the sunlight that we could see it at that great distance. Thinking that was Bill slipping away from house with his Winchester, we ran quickly to the mountain, reaching it in a few minutes.

I told Hofer, Black and Farris to run around the mountain one way, and I started around the other way. We felt sure we had Bill this time, and were so elated that we ran much faster than was necessary, and were traveling at full speed, when we all three reached the man at the same time.

We arrested him and asked him his name.

He said, "I am Rev. Joe Smith, and, as I am going to preach today, I have come out here to pray."

We were dumfounded. Noticing that the large Bible, which Brother Smith carried, had big silver letters on it, we realized that what we thought was Bill James' Winchester was in reality the Holy Bible.

"Brother Smith" showed us their little church, which was situated at the foot of the mountain, and the mountain had obstructed it from our view.

We humbly apologized to the preacher, and he said that he was thankful and glad to know that it was a mistake. He laughingly remarked that he thought his time had come, and said if he could regain his composure he would go on up to the church and preach his sermon.

XIX

INDIANS ON THE WARPATH

While the ranger boys and I were camping on the North Fork of the Red River, still in search of Bill James, we received a call to go about twenty-five miles further up the river, to protect a family who were threatened with extermination by a band of Indians. We were quite busy at that time; for every day, nearly, we had a horse thief or some other bad character to capture.

We went up, however, to see what we could do for the family who had called for help. I took with me two deputy marshals, Jeff Minet and Tom Mason. I also took my rangers, George Black, Jim Farris and Frank Hofer, the latter being the best Indian fighter in the bunch.

When we reached the house, where the family lived who were threatened by the Indians, we learned that a young man had killed an Indian, who had attempted to steal a steer from them. The Indian was armed with a Winchester, and when the young man caught the Indian in the act of stealing, the Indian tried to shoot him, but the boy was too quick for him and shot the Indian, killing him instantly.

The Indians went on the warpath, and sent word to the whites that they would kill everybody on Wolf Creek, and when we arrived upon the scene, we found them in an ugly humor. They had their faces painted up, and had made all necessary preparations to kill out the whole family of the young man who had killed a member of their tribe.

We were there to protect the family, and, in doing so, it was up to us six men to stand off the Indians, which seemed to us an impossible task. We felt like we were going to be killed, but it was our duty to stay there and protect the women and children from the wrath of the Cohuahua Indians. Those Indians looked quite fierce, and, as you may imagine, we looked rather wild too. It didn't feel a bit funny to us, and we certainly felt small when we looked at them. I was not a bit frightened at first, but for three or four days afterward I felt very shaky, and constantly put my hand up to my head to see if I was scalped.

We made peace with the Indians by bluffing them, and making them think we would kill all of them if they attempted to fight us. We did not expect to prevent trouble that easily, and were surprised when we learned that they had decided not not to fight us. It was remarkable that they were so easily subdued. If they had tried, they would have killed us all, and we often wondered why they didn't.

The people, whose lives we saved, were very thankful to us, and when they had recovered sufficiently from their fright they entertained us royally. We were given all the good fried chickens we could eat, and treated as if we were preachers and lords of England.

XX

THE OPENING OF THE CHEYENNE AND ARAPAHOE STRIP

In 1891 the Cheyenne and Arapahoe Strip was opened up to settlers. Billy McCauley, Lon Lewis, John Herrington, Capt. W. J. McDonald and I left Quanah to go to the opening of this strip, knowing that this would be a good place to capture outlaws. We went by Mangum, in Greer County, and got John Byers and John Ovelton and stopped at Oak Creek, which was about nine miles from what was going to be the new county seat—Cloudchief. This territory was to open up at twelve o'clock, and when we reached Oak Creek we got the correct time from one of the soldiers. About twenty-five hundred men were at Oak Creek alone, waiting for twelve o'clock to come.

When the hand of my watch reached twelve, I laid steel to my horse, and we all made a break for the county seat, after crossing Oak Creek, which was about fifty steps from us. Men from all sides of this strip were headed for the new county seat, under full speed. Wild cats, loboes, coyotes, antelopes and badgers were running in every direction. One of our posse roped a deer, and another killed one, while they were all running in every direction. This was about as exciting a time as I ever experienced; horses falling on every side, from stepping in gopher and salamander holes, and dust so thick that a man could hardly see in front of him. Our crowd made the run of nine miles in thirty-five minutes. I staked out two claims, one within a mile, and the other a mile and a half from the county seat.

The signal, which meant that the county seat was open for settlers, was given by a soldier firing a cannon. Up to this time there wasn't a soul to be seen in the new county. In less than thirty minutes after the signal was given this was a solid city covered with tents. We people, who made the run, were to get a business lot and residence lot. I made a mistake and staked a street instead of a lot. I had quite a little argument before they convinced me that I was mistaken. We failed to locate any parties that we wanted and turned back to our headquarters in Quanah.

XXI

A CUP AND SAUCER EVENT

In the fall of 1892 Capt. McDonald discharged the company cook, and each ranger had to do the cooking for a week while in camp. On one occasion it was Ben Owen's week to cook, and, after preparing an inviting breakfast one frosty morning at the camp in Amarillo, he discovered in setting the table that he was short one saucer, and it so happened, when the boys took their seats at the table, that Lee Queen was the man short a saucer, and Queen made some remark about everyone having a saucer but him. Owens shoved his saucer over to Queen, striking his cup and knocked a little coffee out on the table, and, at the same time, remarked, "Here, baby, take this one."

This seemed to offend Queen very much, and he threw the saucer back to Owen, striking his cup, breaking both cup and saucer. Both men jumped to their feet and pulled their guns. I grabbed both men and prevented what might have been a killing over a very small thing. I have always been glad that I was in time to prevent this shooting, and I go on the theory that it is better to be a peacemaker and prevent trouble than to make it. After a few minutes, Owen and Queen saw the folly of their acts, shook hands, and have remained to this day the best of friends.

XXII

A Prisoner Escapes

While stationed at Amarillo I went to Woodward, Oklahoma, after a fellow by the name of Bill Hines, who robbed a man of $600.00 in Collingsworth County. I caught this man, and while we were crossing the Canadian River, about a mile from Canadian City, I dropped off to sleep, as I had been on the go for three days and nights and was worn out. I woke up in Canadian City, and found that Billie had bidden me good-bye while I was asleep, and had struck a stock train and gone back to Woodward, Oklahoma. He had taken this train before I awoke after our train had arrived in Canadian City. This is the only man who ever made his escape from me: I took the train the next morning for Woodward City, but failed to catch Bill.

That day, while I was searching for Bill in Woodward, three prisoners broke jail at this place. I was called on to assist the officers in the capture of these three men. I got in shape at once, and joined the posse. Ex-Sheriff Love and I crossed the Canadian River one mile below where the prisoners had crossed. Tobe Odom and his posse engaged in a fight with Jim Hefner and John Hill, two of the prisoners. We reached them too late to join in the fight. Both of the fugitives were killed. Ben Woodford's right arm was shot off.

George Wattle, the third prisoner, was not with

the party at the time of the fight, but we found him one mile from there lying down on his Winchester. He made no fight, and when called upon to surrender, he threw up his hands at once. Several of the men in the crowd said, "Let's kill him anyhow." I spoke up and said, "If you kill that man I'll hold you responsible for murder, as he has surrendered and thrown up his hands." Temple Houston, who was with us, spoke up and said, "Sullivan, you are right." We sent for a hack and hauled the three men in—two dead, and one alive. We jailed Wattle. This fellow, John Hill, was a very dangerous man. He feared nothing on earth and was known as a slick artist in the Territory in his line of business. Hefner was not so desperate, but all three were bad enough.

XXIII

THE CAPTURE OF RIP PEARCE

I captured one Rip Pearce, charged with hold-holding up a Fort Worth & Denver passenger train, with the intention of robbing the express car. He held up this train in a cut about four hundred yards from the Canadian River, near Tascosa, Texas. Rip Pearce was about thirty years of age at that time, and was six feet two inches and a half tall, and weighed about 200 pounds. When I arrested Pearce he made no fight. I jailed him at Tascosa. I concealed myself at the jail, and did not let him know it. He became awfully restless, and commenced walking the floor and talking to himself. There were no other prisoners in the jail except him. He cried and said, "If I ever live to get out of this scrape, I will always behave myself and lead a different life." When I made him make this remark, I was satisfied that I had the right man.

D. B. Hill was district attorney. I had a hard time locating Mr. Hill, but I kept the wires hot in every direction and finally got word to him, and he arrived just in time to keep Judge Penery from releasing Pearce from the jail on a writ of habeas corpus. Pearce had employed Judge Penery to defend him in his case. Judge Penery was at one time county judge of his county. Pearce knew that the judge was a fine lawyer, and I also found it out before this trial was over.

After Pearce was released he fell in love with a

bunch of horses in Hall County. He fancied these horses, and at last got the consent of his mind to deprive the owner of them, and was captured and sentenced to seven years in the penitentiary. He served his time out, and has been free for several years. I learned that he had reformed and was living a good, honest, upright life, which I was very glad to know.

"Sergeant Sullivan in Camp."

XXIV

A PRACTICAL JOKER GETS INTO TROUBLE

While I was at Amarillo, one Bob Keene, who was traveling from New Mexico to Amarillo, met the stage coming from Plainview to Amarillo. He held the stage-driver up and made him get out of the stage, and, pointing his sixshooter at him, he made the driver dance nearly two hours. After releasing him, Keene forced the driver to drink until he was pretty well under the influence of "Brother Red-Eye." Keene then started on his way, and the driver was satisfied he had gotten rid of him. When he had driven about three miles, however, he heard a noise behind him. He looked around, and Keene threw down on him again, and held him up and had him to cut the "pigeon wing" again. The driver reported Keene as soon as he arrived in Amarillo. I was not in camp at that time, and he reported this to the rangers. Bob McClure, and one or two of the rangers, left at once and followed Keene out to the seven-mile windmill, where he had held the driver up. It commenced snowing and they returned to camp. I came in that night at twelve o'clock off a scout, and they laid this case before me. The next morning I took my saddle horse and one of the State mules and got a buggy, and, with Duncan Meredith, one of the rangers, I started out to find this man. The snow was nearly knee-deep to our team, and covered the ground everywhere in that part of the state and caused us to lose our way several times; but we succeeded in getting out, and about sixty-five miles west of Amarillo, at Jim Ivey's ranch, I captured Bob Keene. He was tried at Fort Graham for holding the stage up and detaining the United States mail, and was fined nearly a thousand dollars.

XXV

Race Thomas is Guarded

I was called by Hughes Tittle, the sheriff of Greer County, to assist him in holding a mob off Jeff Adams and Race Thomas, who had killed McMuse. A mob of one hundred and fifty armed men tried to take these two men from the sheriff as he went to feed the prisoners. Hughes Tittle was such a noble man, and so well-known by this mob for his good qualities and bravery, that the mob would not take his life to get these criminals. Hughes wired me at Amarillo to come and assist him, in case the mob made another break. I went at once, and stayed there two months guarding the jail day and night, but the mob never returned.

Race turned State's evidence, and Adams got a life sentence in the penitentiary, but was held six years in the Quanah jail while the authorities waited to see who had jurisdiction over Greer County—the State of Texas or the United States; but Uncle Sam finally fell heir to the county. Adams went to the penitentiary for life. While in jail Adams used every means to make his escape. I was called on by the jailer of Quanah to help search the jail, when he found where Adams was cutting or sawing. At last we found his saw tied to him on the inside of his clothes. While bringing Adams from Mangum, he and Thomas tried every way possible to pick their shackles when night came on. We had a time getting Adams' shackles and handcuffs off, as he had broken off several toothpicks in the keyholes.

We also held Race Thomas for a witness for six years. Uncle Sam agreed that the State of Texas was entitled to jurisdiction over Greer County at that time. I have not given the full details of this trial, as I do not deem it of importance to do so.

Greer County is ninety miles long and seventy-eight miles wide. It is the largest county known in the world. At that time this county was running over with all kinds of outlaws. While in the ranger service I only searched four caves, one in Greer County, one in the Indian Territory, across the North Fork of Red River, and two in Palo Pinto County. I always felt somewhat lonely while searching these caves.

I was one of the rangers who helped to guard George Isaacs at Quanah, when he was sentenced to the pen for life for killing Tom McGee, the sheriff of Hemphill County, at Canadian City. After he was sentenced I carried him to Fort Worth and jailed him for the contractor at the penitentiary to come and get him. He was pardoned out through a false pardon by a man by the name of Dent, who had served four years in the penitentiary. While in there he got acquainted with Isaacs. This was during Governor Sayers' administration. Governor Sayers was perfectly innocent of knowing anything of this pardon, or anything of Isaacs being out of the pen, until he was notified by Judge Sam Cowan, a lawyer who helped to prosecute him. The officers who helped hold this court and guard Isaacs during the trial, were Fred Dodge; Captain Arrington, one of the old ex-ranger captains; Charlie Stockton; Captain A. J. Paine; three Wells-Fargo men; Dick Cofer, the sheriff of Hardeman County, and myself; also several others—eighteen guards in all.

This is just a small sketch of this. I have not gone into details in this case, as I have in some others. Dent was captured, tried for the killing of Tom McGee, and sentenced to the penitentiary for life, and is now serving his sentence.

XXVI

A SAD FAREWELL

I went to Canadian City one day after two prisoners who were sentenced to the penitentiary. I was called upon to take them to Fort Worth and turn them over to an agent of the penitentiary, who was to take them from there to Huntsville, where the State prison is located.

Reaching Canadian City, I went first to the hotel to get breakfast. As soon as I set my grip and Winchester down, I was approached by two ladies, who asked me if I had come after some prisoners. One of them was an old lady, while the other was rather young looking, and, from the worried expressions on their faces, I took them to be the mother and sister of Jim Long, one of the two prisoners whom I had come after. Long was sentenced to the penitentiary for forging checks on a bank in Canadian City.

Answering their question, I told the women that I had come after two prisoners to take them to the penitentiary. Both of them got up from their chairs and commenced to pacing up and down the floor, sighing and groaning.

After I had eaten breakfast, the old lady told me that she was Jim Long's mother, and that the other lady was his wife. They asked me if they could stay at the jail with Long until the train arrived, and I told them that I thought it would be alright with the sheriff. Getting the sheriff's permission also, they stayed in the jail with the prisoner until nearly train time.

When the time came for me to take the prisoners from the jail, I handcuffed them together, and, with the sheriff and the two ladies, we started for the depot. The strain was too great for Long's wife, and she fainted as we were leaving the jail. Long's mother bore up pretty well under the ordeal, though it was quite an effort, but she did it on account of her daughter-in-law, who fainted two more times before we reached the depot. The old lady couldn't keep the tears back, however, and she walked all the way to the depot with her arms around her son. The sheriff and Long's wife walked behind us, the former trying his best to console Mrs. Long.

When we reached the depot, Long's mother leaned over and whispered to me that she had seventy-five cents at the jail, and that she had given her son twenty-five cents, and wanted to give him the other fifty cents, too. She asked me my advice about it, and I told her to give it to him if she wanted to. She gave the money to him, and when we reached the depot she told me that she and her daughter had return tickets to their home town, but that they owed a four days' hotel bill and had no money to pay it with. They seemed very much distressed about it, but I told them not to worry; that I would see that the bill was paid. I found the proprietor of the hotel in the depot and talked with him about the matter, and he agreed to knock off one-third of the bill. I then paid one of the remaining thirds, and the sheriff paid the other, leaving them free of that debt. We saw that they arrived safely home, and it made us happy to think that we had soothed the broken hearts of two poor, unfortunate women.

XXVII

A Clever Thief is Caught

While at my post of duty in Amarillo, Captain W. J. McDonald told me to take whichever one of the ranger boys I wanted and go to a certain ranch in the Panhandle country and look after some cattle stealing that was alleged to be going on. I took Jeff Madkins, a ranger who had lately been enlisted in the service. I wanted to try his nerve, and I decided that this would be a good place, as this ranch was situated on the Texas and the Territory boundary line, and I knew that we would come in contact with many tough characters before we were through with our work in that part of the State.

This cattle company boarded Madkins and me and our two horses, and gave us forty dollars apiece every month above what the State was giving us. At that time I was corporal and drew thirty-five dollars a month regularly.

Madkins and I rode every day for four months looking for cattle thieves. The superintendent of this ranch and his wife and son, all three, claimed that the nesters were stealing the cattle; so we took particular pains to visit these nesters as often as we could, but failed to find any beef on their tables, or beef bones lying around the place; all the beef that we got to eat would be at the general round-ups. At these round-ups, one of the nesters would kill a calf today, and, in a day or two, another nester would kill one of his calves. Then the superintendent of the ranch would kill a beef.

This superintendent was paying a high tax to the State for so many head of cattle. This English company seemed to have gotten uneasy, for some reason, and sent from Austin, Texas, a man to investigate the condition of their ranch. He and I had a talk. I had at that time been there only two months. I had ridden this pasture out thoroughly everywhere, and had made close a investigation, and I was prepared to answer this man's questions, and he interrogated me rather closely, too. He asked me how many cattle there were on the ranch that belonged to the company. I told him that I had ridden the pasture for two months, and I didn't believe that there could be over fifteen hundred or two thousand head of cattle rounded up in that company's brand.

What I said somewhat vexed this man, and he claimed that the company was paying taxes on eighteen or twenty thousand head of cattle. I told him the cattle were not on the ranch. He then asked me what I thought about the stealing that was going on.

I told him that I thought there was very little stealing going on by the nesters, though sometimes they might slip a calf, but it was seldom.

Then he asked me about the lobo wolves, and I told him that I did not think they were bad; for I seldom ever saw a cow running across the prairie from one high peak to another bawling for her calf, and that I believed I could safely say to him that there was a mistake in regard to the nesters stealing the company out; but, if I stayed there long enough, I would catch the parties who were doing the stealing.

So I remained there two months longer, riding every day. The superintendent was furnished by the company all the horses that he and his wife and son needed to ride, and all the milk cows they wanted. Outside of that, however, they were not allowed to own a horse or a cow on the inside of that pasture. I began to suspect the superintendent, and one day, during a round-up, while I was sitting under a mesquite tree, the horse rangler, who had charge of the remouther, came up and talked with this superintendent for quite a while. It came to my mind, when this fellow rode up, that he might be able to give me some information as to whether the superintendent was acting fairly with the company or not; so I took my day-book out of my pocket, and I told him that the old man and the old lady had promised time after time to give me their brands of the cattle which they owned themselves. This was not so, however, for the superintendent and his wife never had told me that they owned a cow or a calf inside of this pasture. They told me that all the cows that they needed to milk were furnished to them by the company, and the company would not allow them to own a cow and calf inside of the pasture. This remouther rangler dismounted, and took my day-book and wrote down a brand for the old man, a brand for his son, a brand for his daughter, and two brands that they had bought, making six brands the family owned inside the pasture.

I took these brands to the bookkeeper, a nephew of the owner of the ranch, who just had sense enough outside of book-keeping to know that he was human. I asked him if the superintendent had any right to own brands in that pasture. He said that he was not allowed to own even one cow. I showed him the six brands which I had procured from the horse rangler, and asked him if he knew whether that superintendent was running those brands in his pasture. He said he did not know it, and did not think it could be possible. He asked me to give him the brands, which I did, and he sent them at once to England to his uncle. His uncle sent a man at once from England to investigate this matter. The man from England, after investigating the condition of affairs, was thoroughly convinced that the superintendent and his family had stolen this ranch nearly out of cattle; so he fired the whole business off the ranch at once and put another man in his place. The new manager rounded the pasture up from one end to the other, and cut the company's cattle out to themselves and counted them. He got the large sum of eleven hundred and twenty head.

Madkins and I were invited one night by the former superintendent's wife to come up to her house. We accepted her invitation, and when we stepped into her room we hardly knew her, she was dressed in such fine style—diamonds in her ears, diamonds on her fingers, and diamonds on log chain bracelets, and a three-hundred-dollar scarf pin. She and Madkins and I seated ourselves around a beautiful table, while her husband lay on a fine sofa.

Opening the conversation, the lady said, "Mr. Sullivan, what I wanted to see you about is in regard to seven men on the inside of these wires.

This stealing that is going on will never cease until the scalps of these seven men are taken."

She then named the men over to us, and said that there was two thousand dollars apiece for the scalps of these seven men. She said she had the money ready to pay for their scalps as soon as they were turned over to her.

I sat still and said nothing, but listened to her proposition. When she had finished, I looked at her and asked, "Did you aim that proposition at me?"

"Not particularly at you, Mr. Sullivan," she replied, "but at anyone who sees fit to take it up. The money is ready now."

I told her that the State of Texas didn't have me employed to take men's life and property, but to protect them, and that I was going to execute the law in the proper way. "If you or your husband, who is lying over there on the sofa, or your son should violate the laws of our state, I would arrest you as quickly as I would any other criminals."

She saw that I was mad, and she said that she didn't mean her proposition to me, but for anyone who wanted to take it up.

When we left the house, I told Madkins that I was a little too hasty in refusing to consider her proposition. "A character like that," I said, "ought to be in the penitentiary, and, as district court is in session, I shall lay the case before the judge and prosecuting attorney."

I went to town the next morning and saw those two officials, and repeated the whole conversation which took place between the woman and me the night before. I told them that I was going back and take up her proposition, and make her pay me half the money down and take her note for the balance, to be paid when the work was done. "Then I will turn the money over to you, judge," I continued, "and we will prosecute that woman and put her in the penitentiary, where all such characters belong."

The judge and the attorney both spoke up then, and said that I had made her mad and that I couldn't stand in with her any more.

I told them that I could tell the woman that I refused to consider her proposition because she made it to me in the presence of the other ranger, whom I could not trust, since he was a new man in the company and I did not know him well enough. I told them again that I could make a trade with her, and we would get the papers and money for proof and send her to the penitentiary.

Both of them begged me not to interfere with her, saying that she was crazy, or she would not have made that proposal to me. They finally persuaded me not to get the woman into trouble, and I let the case stop where it was.

It seemed, however, that she was bent on getting into the penitentiary before she was through.

A certain man—one of the seven whom she wanted killed—lived in the pasture about a mile from her house. He had been in a shooting scrape with her son a year before, and one evening while sitting in front of my boarding house talking to two other boarders, I saw this man riding from the postoffice to his home. The woman lived about a block from where we were, and the man had to pass her house on his way home.

The woman had often told me that this man was always armed; so on this occasion, as he rode by on his horse, I watched closely to see if I could see the print of his sixshooter. He had on a little blue jumper coat, and I could not see any sign of a gun being on him, though it would easily have made an impression on his little coat if he had been carrying one.

As I was watching him ride slowly up the street, I noticed the woman, with a gun in her hand, standing in the east corner of her yard, just a few steps from where the man whom she hated had to pass in another minute.

I asked the man, who ran the boarding house, how long it had been since the man on the horse and the woman's son had met.

He replied that they had never met since they had the shooting scrape.

I suggested to the men that we watch and see if they speak. As we were on a line with them, we had no difficulty in seeing their movements.

Neither one bowed nor spoke to the other. She watched him, but he never looked to the right nor left. He must have seen her before he reached the house, but while he was passing close by her he never turned his head in her direction, but looked straight in front of him.

When he had passed her, she fired her gun twice across the road. He never even looked around to see if she was shooting at him, but rode straight ahead and soon went out of sight.

It was nearly dark, and we three men were still sitting in the yard, when the woman came down to the gate where we were and asked for me.

I went to the gate, and she proposed that we walk up the road, saying that she wished to talk with me. After walking about forty steps, she turned to me and asked, "Mr. Sullivan, what do you reckon?"

I told her I didn't know.

She then referred to the man whom I had seen on horseback, and said, "I was standing in the east corner of my yard awhile ago, and that dirty villain passed by and jerked out a rubber handled, blue barrel sixshooter and threw it cocked in my face."

I asked her why she didn't scream or notify me, so I could arrest the man and get his gun.

"The reason why I didn't," she replied, "was that I thought it best for you and me to get in my buggy and go to town in the morning, and I will swear out three complaints against him; one for assaulting me with a sixshooter, one for carrying a sixshooter, and I will also have him put under a peace bond."

After telling her I would see her the next morning, I joined the two men whom I left a few minutes before and told them what the woman had said. They said that they had watched every movement that she and the man made when the man passed her house, and that they could swear that the woman's statements were opposite to the truth. I then announced my intention of going to town with the woman, and letting her swear out the complaints against the man. I explained that such a character should be in the penitentiary, and that it was fortunate that there was a way of getting her in there.

The two men, however, begged me not to do that, saying that they did not want to see the woman get into trouble. I laid the case before a merchant, who, I afterward learned, sold lots of goods to this woman, and he begged me not to let the woman perjure herself.

I finally decided, myself, that it was not best to let the woman get into so much trouble, but I went to her house the next morning as I had promised, and asked her if she was ready to go to town.

She said she was ready to go right away and swear out the complaints.

I then told her that two other men besides myself had watched every movement that she and the man made when he passed her house, and that we were ready to swear that her charges were false as soon as she swore to them.

"Mr. Sullivan," she replied, "let's drop the matter where it is, and let it go and say no more about it."

I told her that that was the safest way for her to do; that the penitentiary would have gotten her if she had sworn out those charges against that man.

XXVIII

THE GORDON TRAIN ROBBERY

While at my headquarters I received a message from Adjutant General Mabry at Austin, notifying me that a train was held up on the T. & P. Railroad, four miles east of Gordon, by four train robbers. Superintendent J. V. Goode, of that railroad, gave me transportation for eight men and eight horses and saddles, and I left at once for Gordon, taking with me Bob McClure, Jim Wise, Lee Queen, Billie McCauley, Jack Harwell, Arthur Jones and Vernon Resser, all rangers. We arrived in Gordon that night and put up at the hotel.

The next morning the proprietor of the hotel told me that there was a Jake Smith, who lived in the country, who looked rather suspicious to him. He said that when the train robbery was announced in the hotel, he noticed Jake Smith turning pale and becoming rather nervous. "Jake made the remark," continued the hotel man, "that he bet the robbers had gone north."

I asked the proprietor if Jake ever came to town much, or was it rather unusual for him to be in town and stopping at the hotel. He replied that Jake hadn't been in Gordon before in two years.

We started out early the next morning to the country to look for the robbers. On account of what the hotel man had told me, I went to Jake Smith's house, but before reaching there I procured some more information concerning Smith. I learned, among other things, that two suspicious characters had been staying around Smith's place, and that one of them was wounded and remained there about six weeks. The sick man went by the name of Wilson, and it was presumed that he was shot while robbing some train or store. I was pretty well prepared for Jake when I first reached his house, but I didn't let him know it.

I shook hands with Jake, and told him that I knew very little about the country, and that I wanted him to pilot me to a place called Board Tree Springs. He said he would take me there, and we tramped all day through the rocks and brush, and walked and rode around the many crooks and turns of the Brazos River, not reaching Board Tree Springs until late that evening. He could have taken us there in a half hour if he had wished to do so, as it was only a mile and a half from his house; but Jake did not want to find these springs any sooner than he could help, for he knew that we would discover something there.

When we reached the springs we found four pallets, made of sage grass, spread upon the ground where four men had slept. The pallets were about twenty feet apart, and we saw that they had tied four horses up for a long time.

We learned afterward that the robbers had concealed themselves at this place, and that they waited there for Wilson, the wounded man who stopped with Jake Smith, to get well enough to join them and help them rob the T. & P. train. After Wilson got well they had to wait then for the train that was to bring the money to pay off the coal miners at Thurber.

A little while before the train was to pass by

with its fifty thousand dollars, the robbers captured the section hands and forced them to spread the rails about nine inches. Then they made the hands walk up the track about a hundred yards away from the spreading of the rails, and when the train arrived they ordered Lockerby, the section foreman, to flag it. When the train stopped, the robbers jumped into the express car to take the fifty thousand dollars out, but failed to get it, as the money was in a Thurber safe, which had a time lock on it. They carried off two thousand dollars, however, that they found in another safe which was smaller than the Thurber safe and more easily opened.

The train pulled into Gordon an hour late, and the conductor reported the robbery to the officers, and, as already stated, I was then ordered by Adjutant General Mabry to do all I could to run down the robbers. Governor James S. Hogg was on the train when it was held up.

When we reached Board Tree Springs we found a large bay horse, branded low down on his left thigh with a letter E. This horse was shod with new shoes, but his feet were terribly cut and bruised around the hoofs. They had run him over the hills and rocks until he was unable to travel any longer. The robbers then stole a Paint horse and rode him out and left the bay.

In a live oak thicket, near where the men had done their cooking, I found two boxes, a coffee pot, frying pan, skillet and a water bucket.

Jake Smith claimed that the first day they came to his house there were only two men, and he said they told him that they wanted to find a pasture for twelve or fifteen hundred head of cattle. Jake said that the men borrowed the cooking utensils which we found in the thicket from him. He also explained Wilson's presence in his house, by saying that the latter came to him and claimed to be suffering with a rising, and he felt sorry for him and let him stay in his house.

I also found a nail apron, with sugar in one end of it and salt in the other. A carpenter was working on Smith's house when the two men first took dinner there, and while the wounded man was boarding with Smith. Upon opening the two boxes which I found, I discovered some soda in a lady's dress sleeve, and some new clothes with cost marks still on them. I learned that a store had been robbed about eighteen miles from there, and I notified the merchant of my discovery, and he identified the articles as some of his merchandise and took them back with him. On the two boxes, which we opened, we found written in big letters this warning: "Look out for small-pox."

All this proved to us that the men were guilty, and that Jake Smith had aided them somewhat in their work; so I told Jake that he was under arrest, but I kept him in the mountains eleven days before I took him to jail.

After arresting Smith I went on that evening to Jack Scott's house to arrest him, too. When we arrived at his house, Mrs. Scott informed us that her husband was down at Bill Hitson's, near the river, helping to brand cattle. Our party at that time consisted of eighteen men, and I did not want to take so many to Mr. Hitson's, so I asked Mrs. Scott if she could keep nine men for me that night, and she replied that she could. I left them there, and the other eight men and myself started for Bill Hitson's place.

When we were half way there we met three cowboys, and I spoke to them and asked if one of them was Jack Scott. One man spoke up and said he was Scott; so I put him under arrest and took him back to Bill Hitson's with me, and let the other two cowboys go.

The nine men whom I had left at Mrs. Scott's came up and told me that the two cowboys, who were with Scott a little while before, had reported to Mrs. Scott that I had arrested her husband, and she ordered them off the place, saying that she did not want them to roost under her roof. Hitson had to take care of all eighteen of us, but he did not seem to mind it and treated us nicely.

I didn't let Smith and Scott get together, for I did not want them to "make medicine." I went back to Scott's house the next morning with him, and offered him five hundred dollars if he would tell me the names of the guilty parties, but Scott replied that he did not know any more than I did about the affair. I got him to walk with me back to the bunch of men where Smith was. When we got close enough for Smith to hear me, I said to Scott, "I thank you for giving me so much information about the guilty parties."

I watched Smith closely to see what effect that would have on him. He turned pale at first, and in another minute perspiration began to pour off his face. I looked around over the boys, and acted as if I was quite particular about whom I selected, and told Bob McClure and Lee Queen to guard

Jake carefully; that we surely did not want him to escape. After I had handcuffed Jake, we mounted our horses and rode off, Jake and I riding close to each other.

Jake asked me what Jack Scott had told me. I replied that Scott had informed me that he (Jake) had harbored the men who robbed the store and the express car. He said that Scott was a liar.

I saw all the time that he was worried, and I tried hard to make him break down and give me the names and whereabouts of the robbers, promising to release him if he did so, but he would not do it.

When we reached Smith's house, I left Jake outside with the others, and took Jim Wise, a ranger, into the house where Mrs. Smith, her daughter, and three young men were.

I asked Mrs. Smith if these three men were her sons.

"Two of them are," she replied.

"I want to talk to the oldest one," I said, and she consented.

The young man stepped forward, and I informed him that his father was under arrest for being an accessory to the Gordon train robbery. I told him that his father had informed me that he had let the robbers have a bucket, some cooking utensils, some flour and some meat, but he could not remember whether it was a ham or a shoulder.

"It was a ham," said the boy.

I told him that his father couldn't remember the dates when he did these things, but asked me to see his sons about it, saying they could remember such things better than he could.

"I remember when the things occurred," replied the boy, "but I cannot remember the dates, though I think my brother can give you that information."

I called his brother then, but he couldn't remember the dates either. He, however, also said what I wanted him to. Like his brother, he did not suspect my purpose, and told me that he knew these things happened, but could not remember the dates.

Mr. Smith's family seemed to be very nice people. Mrs. Smith sat still during my conversation with her son, and when I was through with him, I told her that everything pointed to her husband's guilt. She made no reply, but I could tell what she and her children were thinking, from the significant expression on their faces. Their countenances seemed to say in words: "Father, husband, you should not have stood in with Bill, the crippled robber, and, if you hadn't, you would not be in such a bad shape now."

Captain Lightfoot, an officer from Thurber, and I took Smith to Dallas and lodged him in the county jail. When he entered the jail he turned over all the money he had with him, except two dollars, to the jailer. Because he broke into the Dallas County jail with the small sum of two dollars, the jail-birds flogged Smith soundly, and, stripping him, poured a pitcher of icewater on him.

Smith was tried for his part in the robbery, but was acquitted, though the common belief was that he was guilty. McCall, a prominent attorney of Weatherford, represented him.

After disposing of Smith, I returned to the mountains to capture the four robbers. One night while some of us rangers were in a mesquite flat, we looked up and saw four men coming down off a mountain. I told my boys that they must be the robbers, and, when the men got closer, we heard them say something about us being rangers. Then, believing more firmly than ever that they were the robbers, we charged them, but when we arrived within fifty yards of them, a man in the crowd called out to me that he was Sheriff Williams of Young County. They were looking for the same robbers that we were, so we joined forces and went to Hitson's ranch to spend the rest of the night.

We were in a mighty rough country to hunt criminals, and were very much handicapped in that respect. We were told, upon good authority, that there were three hundred and eleven miles of crooks and bends in the Brazos River in Palo Pinto County, while it is only thirty miles straight across. No one can imagine how rough it was up and down that river, unless he has been there long enough to see it for himself. It was hard on us rangers, coming, as we did, off the plains in August and dropping down into these hills, rocks, cat-claws and prickly pears at such a dreadful time of the year.

We learned some time after we first visited Board Tree Springs that there was a cave about seventy-five yards from there which led under a hill. We thought it possible for the robbers to be in that cave; so we entered it and searched thoroughly for the men, but failed to find them. It was such a gloomy looking place in there that we drew straws to see who were to go in, and it fell on Arthur Jones and me. The cave was about seven feet high and eight feet wide, and extended back about a hundred yards. Arthur and I searched every crook and corner, and discovered many rocks, some of them weighing from sixty to a hundred tons. With our sixshooters cocked and ready for action, we looked behind every large rock, and were disappointed every time we failed to find the robbers.

While we were going out of the cave we heard the sound of money and heard the boys outside calling out to us that they had found money. Arthur and I both broke for the entrance, and before we got out we heard one of the boys say, "It's a twenty-dollar bill." Our lights went out, but we did not stop running. We ran into so many rocks, however, that we were skinned up and bruised from head to foot and looked as if we had been in an Irish battle. When we reached the outside the boys gave us the horse laugh, and we were confronted with the cold fact that it was all a joke.

We stayed in that country for some time after that, but were finally forced to abandon our chase, as luck was entirely against us.

XXIX

THE SURRENDER OF FOUR TRAIN ROBBERS

On the night of November 14, 1895, being at headquarters camp at Amarillo, on the Fort Worth & Denver Railroad, I received a telegram from George Leftrick notifying me that six well-armed men, whose actions were suspicious, were camped in Sid Webb's pasture, twelve miles south of Bellview, Clay County, Texas.

I had just returned with seven mounted men from an unsuccessful search, lasting eighteen days, on the Brazos River and in the Palo Pinto mountains, for four men who had held up a Texas & Pacific train, four miles east of Gordon, in Palo Pinto County.

Knowing that a train robbery had been committed at Red Fork some time previously, and suspecting that these men mentioned by Leftrick were the robbers, I took Billy McCauley, Jim Wise, Doc Neeley, Jack Howell and Bob McClure and left for Bellview, shipping our saddles on the train. On arriving within two and one-half miles of Bellview, I got George Thorn, the conductor, to stop the train, and four of us got off, taking our saddles. Concealing ourselves, we sent word to Leftrick by the other men, informing him of our location, and requesting him to come and bring horses for the party.

When Leftrick arrived I asked him to guide us to the house where the six men were. When we had gotten within two and one-half miles of the house, I saw a man on horseback, some distance off; and he discovered us about the same time, and raised his head and watched us. We were riding fast, and I told the boys to slow their horses and I would investigate the man. When I started toward him, he broke, and, when he did so, I motioned to the boys to come on. I soon came to a four-barbed wire fence, which I cut, letting the boys through, who came up just as I finished cutting the wires. I mounted my horse again, and we captured the man after chasing him a mile and a half. He was also wanted; so I arrested and handcuffed him and took him with us to within two hundred and fifty yards of the house where the six men were encamped.

When Leftrick showed me the house I turned the prisoner over to Doc Neeley, one of the rangers, with instructions to hold him there, and, telling the others good-bye, I ran my horse to the house, my men all following. When I reached the house I got off my horse, leaving the reins over his head. I took hold of the door knob, and, as I did so, the men in the house held the knob on the inside and fired two shots through the door, the bullets passing between my legs. I stepped back about four or five feet from the door and ordered the boys to fire through the door, and we emptied our Winchesters and sixshooters. Billy McCauley and Jim Wise were in front of the house with me, and Bob McClure and Jack Harvell and Leftrick were at the back of the house behind a dugout. As I knew the balls we were firing through the door would go entirely through the house, I told Billy McCauley to go behind the house and tell the other three men to come to the front, as they were not needed back there, there being no windows or doors in the back of the house. After we had emptied our Winchesters and sixshooters, McCauley and Wise stepped behind a rock chimney to reload, and I walked backward to an old wagon that stood about twelve steps from and in front of the door of the house. I reloaded my Winchester and sixshooter, watching the house all the time.

By this time the men on the inside had gone up into a loft in the house. We afterward learned that while they were downstairs we shot the hat off one of the men's heads, and a bullet grazed the neck of one of the men, cutting his coat collar and shirt. When they reached the loft they began fighting us from there. After I had reloaded I motioned to Billy McCauley and Jim Wise to come to me. Jim didn't come, but Billy joined me, and asked me what I intended to do. We were then about six feet from the door.

"I am going to break the door down and go in," I said.

"Isn't that very dangerous?" asked Billy.

"Yes," I replied, "but it is just as dangerous here. We have to get them, and that is the only way."

I then broke the door open and sprang into the house, Billy following me. I saw that the floor of the loft was made of plank an inch thick, with no opening except where a ladder led from the bottom floor to the loft. After Billy and I had gotten inside the house, and after I realized our dangerous situation, I told him to go outside or he would likely be killed; for he was a brave young man who

I knew would not desert me. I tried to persuade him to leave the house, for I realized that if he was killed, I would be partly responsible for it,. having asked him to come in the house with me, but he refused to go, and said he was in there to stay, and if I died he would die also.

Just before we entered the house, I placed my left foot on the bottom round of the ladder leading into the loft, threw a cartridge into my Winchester, and shouted to the men above me that I was in there with them. They asked who I was, and I told them my name, and stated that we were Texas rangers and I wanted them to surrender.

Their leader, who went by the name of "Skeeter," then said to me that they would never surrender. I told him I had the house surrounded by my men and there was no chance of escape, but that if they didn't come out and surrender I would set fire to the house and fire them out like rats; while if they surrendered they would not be hurt. One of the men then told me he would give up, and "Skeeter" said to him, "If you surrender, I'll kill you."

"If that man wants to surrender," I said, "and you kill him, I will burn you at the stake." Of course this was a bluff, as far as the burning part was concerned, but I was determined if this man wanted to surrender he should not be hurt.

"I am coming," said the man who offered to surrender.

"Be quiet while I talk to you," I replied. "Let me see your hands up to your elbows before I see your body, or you are a dead man. Don't attempt to deceive me and try to take advantage of me, for

I have the advantage of you. I have a cartridge in my Winchester, my finger on the trigger, and my hammer gone after fire."

"Here I come," he said.

"Let me see your hands up to your elbows first," I replied.

He did so, and I arrested him, and also arrested the other men in the same manner, and turned them over, one by one, to Billy McCauley as I arrested them. When I had finished, we went outside the house to the spot where I left Doc Neeley, about two hundred and fifty yards away, with the other prisoner. I took the handcuffs off this man and handcuffed the two strongest men together.

My horse, and those of nearly all my men, ran away during the fight. I had a pair of handcuffs and a pair of shackles in my saddle packets. I had one of the rangers go after the horses, and he found them nearly four miles away from where we were, in the corner of a barbed wire fence. When he returned, we hitched the prisoners' horses to a little wagon and took the prisoners to Bellview, and that night we put them on the train and took them to Wichita Falls. Besides the men, we also captured six Winchesters, four sixshooters, eight belts, one thousand rounds of cartridges, twenty-five California blankets, and a new saddle and bridle they had stolen from a man by the name of McDermott.

The man who owned the house in which we captured the men, asked Cooper Wright, the sheriff of Clay County, if he could not recover damages from the State on account of his house being shot and torn up; but the sheriff advised him to keep quiet, stating that if I heard he was talking of making a complaint against me, I would arrest him for allowing such characters to stay in his house, and he took this advise.

The four men, whom we captured, belonged to Bill Cook's party of six. The other two men, Bill Cook and Jim Turner, at the time of the capture of the four men mentioned above, had left the camp before we arrived, in order to locate a place where they could hold up the Fort Worth & Denver train, and also the Rock Island train, on the 17th day of November, 1895. When I arrested the four men at the camp, Bill Cook and Jim Turner were on the way back to camp, having perfected their plans to hold up the two trains, and were within a half mile from the camp at the time of the fight, but upon hearing the shooting they thought it best not to come to the camp.

The four men whom we captured were tried at Fort Smith, Arkansas, for the two train robberies and a postoffice robbery. Charley Turner turned State's evidence and his case was dismissed, but the other three men plead guilty and were sent to Sing Sing for thirty and twenty years each. We got eight hundred and fifty dollars for their capture.

"BILL COOK"

The noted Train Robber—Sentenced to prison at Albany, N. Y.
Served five years and died.

XXX

THE PURSUIT OF BILL COOK AND JIM TURNER

Immediately after the trial of the four robbers whom we captured in Sid Webb's pasture, I got my men together and started out after Bill Cook and Jim Turner. I went to Jack County, and while searching in that part of the country I went to the home of a Mr. Snyder. Jim Turner's father was living there at that time, he being Mrs. Snyder's brother. When my men and I reached the house, Mr. Snyder, Mr. Turner and another man came to the door, and I told them to come to where I was, which they did. I asked them if Bill Cook and Jim Turner were in the house, and they told me there was no male person in the house. I told my men, however, to stay where they were and hold these three men, and I would search the house.

When I reached the door Mrs. Snyder told me to leave my Winchester out of doors, but I told her to please step out of the door, and she did so. I entered the house, searched one room, but found no one. When I entered the room where Mrs. Snyder was, I noticed a large object under the cover of a bed in that room, and there was a small part of the brim of a hat visible from under the edge of the cover. I had my Winchester in my right hand, and with my left I jerked the cover back. As I did so, the fellow swore he would fight every one of us, and used profane language to give weight to his words. When he made this remark I cocked my Winchester and placed the end of it in his mouth. My men heard this man when he spoke, and heard the rattle of my Winchester, so they rushed in. Mrs. Snyder was wiping out a heavy tin biscuit pan, and when she saw my boys coming in, and saw the dangerous position of the man in the bed, she hit me over the head as hard as she could with this pan, and said to me, "You came near killing my son." When I collected my wits and got my hat back on my head, I told my men to go to my horse and get my handcuffs and shackles, and that I would handcuff this man and shackle the old lady, and take them to Jacksboro. She told me if I would not arrest her she would sit down and behave herself, and I told her if she would do so, it would be alright. The three men then came to the door, and Mr. Turner fell and asked Mrs. Snyder for the camphor, saying he had palpitation of the heart. I said to him, "You old villain, you told me such a lie, I have a good notion to give you palpitation of the head." He then said that that man in the bed was Mrs. Snyder's son, but that he had forgotten about him being in the house; that he had been to Bowie, gotten drunk, and they thought my men and I were officers from Bowie who had come to arrest him. I then released this man and left, having seen nothing of Cook and Turner.

On December 22, 1896, I received a letter from J. H. Harkey, sheriff of Dickens County, stating that there were two suspicious characters in his town (Dickens), and from the descriptions he gave I was confident that they were the two men I wanted. My men and I went to Childress, shipping our horses, and then rode from there across the country to Dickens, one hundred and twenty-five miles away. When we arrived at Dickens, Sheriff Jeff Harkey again described the two men to me, and I was still more confident that they were the two men I was after. The sheriff said they had left Dickens and had gone to Scurry County. He consented to go to Scurry County with us, which was one hundred and twenty-five miles from Dickens. After we arrived in Scurry County we went to Mitchell's ranch—the Square and Compass, by name—which was about fifty miles southwest of Snyder, Scurry County. Here we received information from John and Jim Mitchell in regard to Bill Cook, alias Mayfield, and Jim Turner, and they told us the two men had been at their ranch, but that they had gone to Green Igold's ranch, one hundred miles from there.

I had sent back all but two of my men at Dickens, keeping Billy McCauley and Vernon Resser. Deputy Sheriff Ira Gooch joined me at Snyder, Scurry County. Norman Rogers, the sheriff of Kent County, also joined me. Sheriff Harkey left me eight miles from Gail, Borden County; his horse being sick.

When I started to Green Igold's ranch, I had with me only three men, Sheriff Rogers, Deputy Ira Cooch and Vernon Resser, Billy McCauley being forced to stop at Pete Scroggin's ranch, his horse having given out. When we reached Igold's ranch we hitched our horses and started to the house, where we saw Igold standing in the door and five men standing at the window. I told my men to keep an eye on the parties at the window while I had a talk with Igold. When I started toward Igold he said that I must leave my Winchester out of doors. I told him to get out of the door, which he did, and I entered the house. I asked him if those were his men standing at the window, and he replied that they were. I then asked him if Jim Dillard was there, and he said he was. I told Dillard to step out of the crowd, which he did, and I arrested him, as he was wanted at Colorado City for "shooting up the town." He and Joe Elkins and Jim Turner had been arrested by a deputy sheriff at Colorado City, but they had escaped.

I learned from Igold and his men that Cook and Turner had been there, but had left several days before. I took Jim Dillard and started back to Pete Scroggin's ranch, where we were to spend the night. On the way there I met Joe Elkins, who was with some cowboys driving a bunch of cattle. I arrested him, also, and took him with me to Scroggin's.

The next morning I told these two men if they would tell me where Bill Cook and Jim Turner went when they left Igold's ranch, and their plans, that I would release them. They accepted this proposition, and told me that Cook went to Roswell, New Mexico, and Turner went to Colorado City to meet his sweetheart, Zettie Sweezer, where they were to be married; that Bill Cook's sweetheart and his sister were to join him at Roswell, and that Turner was captured in Colorado City, but made his escape. The young lady afterward located him, and they were married in Big Springs, and went to Roswell. They lived there three months, when Turner was arrested and jailed at Fort Smith, Arkansas.

When I was at Mitchell's ranch, as stated, I learned that there was a letter in the postoffice at Grassland, Texas, in care of the Square and Compass ranch, for Jim Turner. My men and I were almost broken down, so I got John Mitchell to get the letter for me, of which the following is a copy:

"ROSWELL, N. M., Dec. 25, 1894.

"MR. JAMES TURNER,

"GRASSLANDS, LYNN CO., TEX.

"Sir: We received your letter yesterday that you wrote to Santie. You wanted to know where he is. He left here last May, and started to the Indian Territory. We have some kinfolks there. We have never heard of him yet. I will close. Mama said she would write to you, but she is getting very old, and cannot see. Hope you all have good luck. It seems like I know you; I have heard Santie speak of you so much.

"Yours respectfully,

"DELLA HARRIS,

"ROSWELL, CHAVES CO.,

"NEW MEXICO."

When I captured Bill Cook's four men, as I have already related, I found on one of them a list of fourteen men who had participated in four robberies with Bill Cook. One of the names on the list was Santie Harris. By getting the above letter, I obtained a clew as to Harris' whereabouts, and it also led me to believe that if Bill Cook was in Roswell, as I had been informed, he would likely be at the Harris home, or, if not there, they could doubtless tell me where he was.

My men and horse were completely worn out; so I took them to Colorado City, and sent them by rail to headquarters at Amarillo. I then went to Roswell, but to keep from attracting attention, I went alone to the courthouse, where I spent the day, having my dinner brought to me, so I would not be seen during the day. When night came on I asked the sheriff if he knew a family in Roswell by the name of Harris, and he answered that he did. About eight o'clock that night I asked him to show me their house. He went with me until we were about seventy yards from the house. Then he stopped and pointed it out to me, but would go no further. After telling him to wait for me at the courthouse, I entered the gate at the Harris home, and was about to close it when a man came up, and I asked him if Mrs. Harris lived there, he replying that she did, as she was an aunt of his. I asked him to tell her I wished to speak to her, and, after he had done so, she came to the door and asked me in, but I told her I preferred to talk to her at the gate. She then came to where I was standing and told me she was Mrs. Harris. I told her my name was Bob Turner, Jim Turner's brother; that Jim had promised to meet me at her house, and a friend of mine by the name of Williams, or probably Mayfield, had also promised to meet me there, and if my friend had been to her house, she had likely learned that the names Williams and Mayfield were his aliases, and she had probably learned his real name. She replied, saying that my brother Jim had not been there, but my friend had been, and that his real name was Bill Cook; that he had arrived there Thursday at noon, and left Friday morning before sunrise. I asked her if he told her to tell me where to meet him, and she said he didn't mention Bob's name, but said to tell brother Jim to meet him at a ranch, the name of which she had forgotten, but it was just to the right of White Oaks. I then told her that some of our party had been captured on the Texas and the Indian Territory line, and also said I had heard her son, Santie, speak of her daughter very often. The man I met at the gate and Mrs. Harris' daughter were in the house, and heard me make the remark about Santie speaking of his sister, and they then came to the door and the man said, "this is Della, now." I then told her about seeing her brother, and Mrs. Harris asked me where I saw Santie. I replied that he joined us last May, and she then denied his ever being out of New Mexico, but said he was then about fifty miles from there, with his father, herding cattle. The man and the girl standing in the door then spoke up and said, "Why, mother, you ought to be ashamed to tell that man that; he is alright," but she told them to keep quiet. I said I would not argue about Santie, but I would like for them to show me the way to White Oaks. I then shook hands with all of them, and asking them not to mention having seen me, I started toward the mountain.

After I had gotten out of sight, I turned and went to the courthouse, where I explained to Perry all that I had learned from Mrs. Harris in regard to Bill Cook, and told him to get a buggy and a pair of the best horses he could find, and we would go to White Oaks on the following morning and capture Cook, White Oaks being one hundred miles from Roswell. I told Perry I had been following Cook so long that I was completely worn out, and I had to have some sleep that night before I could go to White Oaks, but that I would be ready to go with him at daylight.

The next morning I learned that Perry had gotten another man and left for White Oaks that night about midnight. If I had been in my own jurisdiction, I would have gone to White Oaks that morning alone, but being outside the Sate of Texas, I had to have the assistance of some New Mexico officer before I could arrest a man. I therefore asked ex-sheriff Billy Adkins to go with me to White Oaks, explaining to him the way Perry had treated me, and he said he would be glad to accommodate me, as I had assisted him in Texas several times, but that if he did so it would cause trouble between him and Sheriff Perry.

Being unable to get anyone to go with me to White Oaks, I decided to go to El Paso, thinking it probable that Perry would not find Cook, and that he (Cook) would go to El Paso. At Eddy I learned that a man had been placed in jail there a short time before; so I stopped over, thinking, perhaps, this man was Jim Turner, as I was told he was heavily armed; but on going to the jail I found he was not Turner, but was a man whom I had seen at Thurber, Texas, some time before.

The train having left me, I had to stay in Eddy until the next morning, and that night the sheriff and I searched Eddy and another small place a mile from there, thinking we might find Jim Turner, but we failed to do so.

The next evening I left for El Paso. Captain J. H. Hughes was camped at Ysleta, twenty miles from El Paso, and I wired him to meet me at the train and go to El Paso with me, wihch he did. We made a thorough search, both in El Paso and across the river—in Old Mexico, but did not find Cook. That night I heard that Cook had been captured at White Oaks by Sheriff Perry; but it was no surprise to me. I boarded the east-bound train and went back to Pecos, where I met the train Cook was on. I found him with Perry, Tom Love and one McMurray, of Colorado City. Perry was standing on the platform of the train, and I went up to him and said, "You have treated me worse than any honorable officer would treat another." I also told him that was a dirty game he played on me in Roswell. He did not say a word, went into the car where Cook was. I followed him and saw Cook in chains, facing me. I spoke to him, calling him by his name, and he said, "Howdy, John L." On my asking him how he knew me, he replied he had had me described to him very often. Then he wished to know how I happened to recognize him, and I told him I had had his description a long time, but that I believed I would not have known him if it had not been for the squint in his left eye.

Perry and his men had walked back to the rear of the car, and Cook said to me: "Those men have gone back there to 'make medicine' against you; for they have all said they intended to beat you out of the reward and honor of my capture, which I think you justly deserve, for you have simply lived on my trail."

"Is your Winchester a .45-.90?" he then asked.

"Yes," I replied.

"Well, that is my gun, and I suppose you captured it when you captured my four men. I bought four of those guns at the same time, one for myself, one for brother Jim, one for Cherokee Bill, and one for Jim French, costing me eighteen dollars at the factory."

"Where were you at the time I captured your four men?" I asked

"I was about half a mile from you. Jim Turner and I had been out planning to rob the Fort Worth & Denver and the Rock Island trains, and were just returning to camp. Didn't you find a money sack made of ducking, with a train bellcord worked in the top like a tobacco sack? We were going to put the money in that sack when we held up the trains."

"Yes, I found it," I replied, "I have it at my camp."

I then said to Cook, "Bill, you know you are done for now, and you will never be free again. Tell me where Jim Turner is."

"Jim left me at the Z-L ranch," he replied, "and went to Colorado City to meet his girl, and we were all to get together later on and go to Old Mexico. This girl's name was Zettie Sweezer. That is all I know about Jim."

"Why didn't you and Jim help your men when we captured them, if you were only half a mile away?"

"Well, we had left our Winchesters at the camp when we went out to plan for the hold-up, so we would not attract attention, and had only our pistols with us, and decided it was best not to come up without anything but our sixshooters. If I had had my Winchester, I could have easily killed you eight hundred yards away. We met an old gentleman and two ladies in a wagon. The ladies had fainted, and the old gentleman was fanning them. The man said to us, 'You men are strangers to me, but don't go where you hear that shooting, for they are having one of the biggest fights I ever saw; they made my horses run away." Jim and I afterward scouted around in Jack, Palo Pinto, Clay and Dickens Counties, keeping on the move all the time."

When the train arrived in El Paso, I stepped in the depot to put my Winchester and overcoat away, and when I came out I saw that Perry and his men were taking Cook away in a carriage. After they had gone up the street a short distance, they opened the window and looked out. I got a carriage and passed them. They had stopped, and the reporters were writing down every word Cook said.

I drove to the Wells-Fargo Express office and wired to three friends of mine at Kansas City, Simpson, Stockton and Ed Dodge, who were in the employ of the Wells-Fargo Express Company, stating that I was in El Paso; that Bill Cook had been captured, and explained how the three men had ruled me out of the reward entirely, and that I wished to put in my claim for my part of the reward. I only asked for one-fourth of the reward. In about an hour I received a telegram stating that they recognized my claim in full. I have never received any part of this reward.

XXXI

A MISERABLE NIGHT

On the 11th of January, 1895, I went to Eddy, New Mexico, in search of Jim Turner, Bill Cook's right hand man. I happened to be short of money on that day, so I went to a cheap, but respectable hotel to get lodging for the night. I met the lady who ran the house, and asked her if I could get a good room. She said that all the rooms were taken, and then asked me if I would not sleep in a room with Judge Wright. I asked her what kind of a man he was, and she replied that he was a "fine gentleman." I then told her that I would sleep in the room with him.

After engaging the room, I left the hotel and joined the sheriff in the search for Turner, the train robber. About twelve o'clock that night I returned to my room, and went straight to bed. There was no one in the room, and I soon fell asleep, for I was considerably fagged out.

I had been asleep about half an hour when a man entered the room and woke me up with his racket. I turned over and watched his movements for a while in silence. He lit a lamp, and when I got a glimpse of his face I decided that he didn't look much like a lawyer to me. He staggered across the room and sat down on the side of his bed. Then he pulled out his revolver, and, half cocking it, threw it over against the wall.

When he got through I asked him what his name was. He did not tell his name, but replied that he was the deputy sheriff from Tongue River. I told him that he was making an awful play with his sixshooter, and that even if he was the deputy sheriff from Tongue River, he had better go a little slower. I remarked that there were women and children in the next room, and that they would be safer if he kept his sixshooter still. He then attempted to enter into conversation with me, but I told him I was too sleepy to talk any more.

I went back to sleep after he had turned the light low, but nearly an hour after that I was again rudely aroused by another man coming noisily into the room. This time it was the lawyer who had been recommended to me as a "fine gentleman." His face was red, and, like the deputy sheriff, he also threw his feet high when he walked. Getting his clothes off seemed rather a difficult task to him, and I thought he would never accomplish it. When he finally did get undressed, however, he had an equally hard job getting in his bed. He and the deputy sheriff slept in the same bed, and I was frequently disturbed during the night by them getting up to get a drink of water. About five o'clock in the morning, the lawyer made one of his regular dives at his bed, but this time he went the wrong way and landed on top of me. I jumped up, and, grabbing him by the collar, I led him to his bed and pitched him head first on top of the deputy sheriff. Then I dressed and went to a "three-dollar hotel" and paid a dollar for a bed until breakfast.

XXXII

MY EXPERIENCES WITH A BEARSKIN OVERCOAT

When I went up to Eddy, New Mexico, to look for Jim Turner, I took with me my big bearskin overcoat, as the weather had turned very cold. My overcoat was a "scary" looking thing, but I did not realize it when I first got it, so much as I did later on, after I had had a number of unusual experiences on its account.

I was wearing the coat one morning while standing on one of the street corners in Eddy. I had my mind on something rather important to me then, and was not thinking about my coat, when suddenly a horse driven by a man and lady commenced shying at me, and backing off as if it wanted to get as far away from me as possible. I was not enjoying the thought of anything being frightened at me, but suddenly remembering my coat, I got out of sight as quickly as possible. My movement did no good, however, for the horse kept up his rearing and pitching until he had turned the buggy over and damaged it in several places. The occupants of the buggy, fortunately, were not hurt, but I regretted the accident, and, feeling that I was the cause of it, I humbly begged their pardon, and then walked away, hoping that my coat would not get me into any more scrapes like this.

After walking several blocks away from the scene of the first accident, I met a lady carrying a baby in her arms. Following her was her little boy of five years, with his large bull dog at his side.

As soon as the dog spied me he made a grab for my coat. He looked fierce, and I knew it wouldn't do to let him get the advantage of me; so I drew my sixshooter and placed the end of it in the brute's mouth. The woman screamed, and asked me not to shoot the dog. I did not want to kill him unless I was forced to, but he struggled so hard to get to me that I had to keep the pistol in his mouth and walk backward. I told the woman if she would call the dog off I could get away without having to hurt it, but she was too excited to listen to my proposition, and continued to plead for her dog's life. She said he was her only protection when her husband was gone, and that he was a good companion for her little boy. That might have been true, but she could not see any further than that, and could not realize that there was another side to the situation. I told her that the fact that the dog was valuable did not make it impossible for her to take him off me, and let me go on; but she did not look it at in that light, and I had to back down the street until I reached the courthouse steps before I could get rid of the brute.

A woman and a dog following me down the street was quite an event to me, and all because of my overcoat. That was satisfactory to me so far as the lady was concerned, but I would rather not have a woman and a dog both to deal with at the same time. It wasn't long after that, however, until my overcoat caused a lady to run away from me.

I was in Fort Worth, having just returned from Thurber, Texas, to which place I had taken fifty thousand dollars from Dallas, so the miners could be paid off. Col. Hunter, the president of the mines, had requested me to do this, as robberies had become quite numerous.

It was still very cold, and I had on my bearskin overcoat. Early one morning, while riding on a street car, sitting in the corner next to the window, an old lady came in and sat down by me. She failed to see me at first, but when she did chance to look in my direction, she gave a scream that startled everybody on the car, and before anyone could reach her, she ran out of the door and jumped off.

The conductor stopped the car, and asked her what the trouble was. She replied that she did not want to ride with a bear. The conductor assured her that I was no bear; that I only had on a bearskin overcoat.

She came back in, and looked cautiously over her glasses at me, and, giving another unearthly yell, she quickly fled and left the car again. The conductor tried to pacify her, and told her that I was only a Texas ranger wearing a bearskin overcoat; but she said: "I am satisfied that he is a bear. John told me when I left Tennessee that I had better be careful and watch out, for there were lots of strange things down in Texas, and you bet Mary is going to obey John." We went on then, and left Sister Mary standing by the side of the track still obeying "John."

My overcoat was quite comfortable in cold weather, but I was getting tired of the trouble that it was constantly causing me. Still, I had hopes that it would get me into no more scrapes, and kept on wearing it that night.

The next morning I put it on again, and, as I left the hotel to go down town, I passed a little girl, who was about nine or ten years old, standing on the front gallery of her home. Upon seeing me, she called to her mother, telling her to come quick and "see Santa Claus."

While that experience was not so embarrassing as the others, it gave a hint that I was to always have trouble with my overcoat; so I made a solemn vow to sell it as soon as possible, for, on its account, many visions were haunting my mind. Among other things, there was the buggy and horse incident, the bull dog, the little girl and Santa Claus, and an old lady standing by the track obeying "John."

XXXIII

A LIVELY CHASE

While generally successful in arresting noted criminals—although often after a long chase with a battle at the end of it—sometimes when the man sought for was almost within my grasp, he eluded capture. A case of this kind was my pursuit of two men who had held up a Forth Worth & Denver train four miles west of Childress, Childress County, Texas.

In the latter part of 1894, while on the way from Amarillo to San Saba to appear in court against some cattle thieves whom I had arrested in San Saba County, the train which I was on met, at Bowie, a train on which was Walter Lyons, a cattle inspector, who asked me to meet him at Canadian City as soon as possible to assist him in arresting some cattle thieves.

The next morning I heard, while in Fort Worth, that a train on the Fort Worth & Denver Railroad had been held up, but I could get no confirmation of the report. Upon arriving at San Saba, however, I found that the report was true. As soon as my business in court at San Saba was finished, I hurried to Childress to hunt for the robbers.

At Wichita Falls I saw City Marshal Charles Landers, of Vernon, who had come there on the same business that I came for, and also Bill Ish, ex-deputy marshal. They told me that in Vernon, the previous day, they had seen a stranger, riding and driving three horses, one of which was packed, and they had intended to investigate him, but he left sometime during the night and they lost his trail; that they went to Wichita Falls the next morning, hoping to find him there. They also told me that they saw him from the car window as they were coming to Wichita Falls, and he was then driving only two horses.

When they told me this, I proposed going back on the next train and riding until we met him, as he probably would not come to Wichita Falls. After some discussion, this plan was agreed to. When we boarded the train the conductor gave me permission to pull the bell-cord and stop the train if I saw the man. After going about seven miles I saw him and stopped the train, and George Thorn, the conductor, ran the train back as far as he could without placing the sleeper in danger if there should be a fight.

My two men and I then got off and arrested him. Upon searching him, we found papers showing that he had been arrested at Harrell, and that he had been arrested for carrying a pistol, and had paid twenty-two dollars in cash and left the missing horse as security for the balance of the fine. He gave his name as Farmer, from Turkey Creek, Greer County, claiming to be on his way to Denton County after some horses he had there. I asked him why he had so many horses with him when he was going after more of them, and he replied that he did not want to ride the same one all the time. All this took some time, and the engineer kept ringing the bell and blowing the whistle to hurry us, as the train was late. Although satisfied that the prisoner had stolen the horses which he had, I was without proof, and, not believing him to be implicated in the train robbery, I released him, and got back on the train and went to Iowa Park.

Farmer had, apparently, told us a straight story, but I became suspicious after reaching Iowa Park, and Bill Ish and I got a buggy and went back and re-arrested him, searching him carefully, giving his papers a closer inspection and questioning him fully as to himself and his movements. He stuck to his story of going to Denton County after horses, and, although still suspicious, we were unable to make anything of him and again released him, and returned to Iowa Park, where we spent the night at Scott Butler's hotel.

I desired to be called in the morning in time for the west-bound local, and, while sitting in the sitting room that morning, a stranger came in. He seemed to be chilled through, as though he had spent the night out of doors, and I asked him if he had camped out. He said no; that he had spent the night at the section house, a mile or so down the road. I asked him what he had done with his horse.

"What horse?" he said.

"The one you were riding," said I.

"That was a pony. I left him at Decatur two years ago, with Ridley," he replied.

"I am not talking about two years ago;" said I, "I am talking about the horse you rode to the railroad."

"Oh; that horse. I sent him to Greer County."

"What did your partner do with his?" I asked.

"He sent his also," he replied.

I asked him if both horses were bays, and he said, "No; they are both grey."

Upon asking him what he had done with his saddle and bridle, he said he had none; that he had ridden his horse bareback with a hackamore. This made me more suspicious than ever, and I asked him what his partner had done with his saddle and bridle. He said he had sold them to a man at the cement works, four miles west of Quanah.

In answer to my question, he said his name was John D. Hobart and his partner's name was Bill Hughes, and he had known the latter for eleven years in Brown County. Further questions brought out the fact that he had separated from Hughes near the railroad dam, east of the flour mill, in Quanah, about three days previously.

"When you left Bill," I asked, "where did you tell Bill to write to you?"

"I didn't tell him," said he.

"Where did Bill tell you to write him?"

"He didn't tell me."

"Did you shake hands when you parted?"

"No."

"Why not? Had you quarreled?"

"No; we were friends."

"What; you had known each other eleven years, and you had parted without telling each other where to write and without even shaking hands, although you had had no quarrel? I will have to arrest you," I said.

Breakfast was announced about this time, and Landers, Ish and I, together with the prisoner, ate breakfast, and afterward boarded the train and went to Vernon where Hobart was jailed.

From Vernon I wired to Captain J. V. Good, superintendent of the Fort Worth & Denver Railroad, to send the engineer and fireman of the train which was held up near Childress to identify the prisoner.

They came; but were unable to swear positively that he was the robber, as his face was masked at the time of the hold-up. They said, however, that his build, clothes and hat corresponded to those of the robber, as, also, did his voice.

I then took my prisoner to Childress and jailed him, leaving Ish and Landers at Vernon.

When I arrested Hobart, I told him he was arrested for train robbery. He said that on the evening of the robbery he was digging a cellar for Pat Leonard, twenty miles south of Childress.

After jailing Hobart at Childress I went to Amarillo, telling him I would return in the morning and take him out to Leonard's to see if his story as to the cellar could be verified.

On arriving at Childress, the following morning, I was met by a deputy sheriff, who told me that Hobart's story was true, and that he had seen him dig in the cellar on the day he claimed, and that it would have been impossible for him to have reached the scene of the hold-up at the time it took place. Acting upon this, I had Hobart released from jail, and gave him five dollars and a ticket to Iowa Park.

That was the last I ever saw of Hobart, although I afterward tried every way I could think of to find him.

The robbery for which I had arrested Hobart was committed within a few miles of Childress, and the local officers had not succeeded in arresting the robber; so when I found, too late, that there was no truth in the story of either Hobart or the deputy sheriff as to Hobart having been at Pat Leonard's on the day of the robbery, I was compelled to believe that the deputy sheriff had secured his release through jealously over the fact that the robber had been arrested by a ranger after the county officers had failed.

When I released Hobart at Childress, I took the train and went to Amarillo, where I had to appear in court against three cow thieves, a Mr. Swen and his two sons.

The next morning I went to the postoffice and found a letter to me from the jailer at Vernon. Inside of the envelope was another letter written by John Hobart to his uncle at Monktown, Fannin County, in which he made a full confession of the robbery. I succeeded in getting Judge Wallace and Judge Plemons and District Attorney D. B. Hill to release me that evening; for I showed them this letter, and explained to them that I wanted to follow Hobart.

The next morning I started to Decatur, and, upon reaching there, I inquired at the livery stables to find out if Hobart had hired a horse at any time, but found that he had not done so. I found, though, that he had registered at one of the hotels as John D. Hobart, Honey Grove, Fannin County.

I then boarded the train and went to Honey Grove. When I reached that place I went to a merchant, in whom I could confide, and asked him if he knew anyone in the vicinity of Monktown by the name of George Hobart. He stated that he did, and that Monktown was eighteen miles from there, on the Red River; that George Hobart was running a big cotton gin at that place. I asked him if he knew of anyone at Monktown whom I could trust, and he told me that Deputy Sheriff White of that town was a trustworthy man. I went to Monktown that evening, and the next morning I hunted up Mr. White and explained the case to him, and, after describing Hobart to him, I asked White to go out to George Hobart's and see if John Hobart was there. I also told him that if he failed to find him, to tell his uncle, George Hobart, that he had met his nephew three months ago at Decatur, and had been informed by him that there was a man there who had some horses and mules for sale, and that he wanted to know the name of the man with whom his nephew lived in Decatur, so that he could find him and get some information from him in regard to the party who had the horses and mules to sell. White immediately went out to George Hobart's place and saw him, but failed to find the man whom we wanted. He returned, however, with the information that John Hobart lived nine miles from Decatur with a man by the name of John Ridley.

I went to Fort Worth and wired Sheriff Moore of Decatur, asking him if he knew a man by the name of John Ridley in that country, and if he did to meet me at the depot on the arrival of the next train from Fort Worth, with horses and saddles for us both. He answered that there were two brothers, Jim and John Ridley, living nine miles from Decatur; so when I arrived at that town, Moore was waiting for me with horses and saddles

We left at once for Ridley's, and, on the way there, Moore informed me that he had a friend who lived between the two Ridley brothers, and that we had better see his friend first, as we might obtain some information from him.

We called by and saw this man, who informed us that he had been at Jim Ridley's the evening before and at John Ridley's that morning, and that he had not seen anyone who fitted the description of John Hobart. He said, however, that he did see such a person in Decatur the Friday before, with John Ridley and his wife. After we left this man, I suggested to Moore that I go to Ridley's and spend the night, and tell them I was hunting land to rent, but he would not agree to that. We decided to return to Decatur then; for, as court was in session at Decatur, Sheriff Moore had to be there.

The next morning I went to John Ridley's, and, when I knocked, a lady came to the door and informed me that she was Mrs. Ridley.

"Is your husband here?" I asked.

"No, sir," she replied, "if you came from town, you met him not far back."

"I did meet a man about two miles back," I answered, "and I suppose he was your husband."

I then told her I lived on Denton Creek, where I was feeding two thousand beeves. "I heard in Decatur," I continued, "that there was a young man with you and your husband last Friday, and that he wanted to hire to you, but the party who told me didn't know whether you hired him or not, and if you did, he said he didn't think you needed him, and as I am needing help very badly in giving attention to my cattle, I would like to hire him, if he is here and you do not need him."

"That was John Hobart," she replied, "but you would not want him on your place as he is such a vulgar man."

"No; I don't want him," I replied, "if he is a tough character, for I have a wife and four grown daughters."

"He is a right tough character," she said.

"But in case I am forced to have him," I said, "where do you think I could likely find him?"

"I expect you will find him at his grandfather's, who lives on Emerson's prairie, eighteen miles from Paris. His grandfather is named Sol Hideman. John Hobart has one hundred and fifty acres of land at his grandfather's, and he is probably there attending to it."

In the letter which John Hobart wrote to his uncle, which was sent to me by the jailer at Vernon, and in which he confessed to the robbery, he stated to his uncle that he supposed this jail business would make his "cake all dough" with his girl; so I asked Mrs. Ridley if he had a girl, and she replied that he did; that her name was Emma Kitchens, and that she lived on Emerson's prairie.

After gaining this information, I returned to Decatur and went to Paris, hired a buggy and team, and went out to Emerson's store, where I learned the way to Mr. Hideman's. When I reached there, I introduced myself to him under another name, and stated to him that I was renting land south of Paris, but that I had accumulated enough money to buy me a home; that I met his grandson about three months ago, and he told me he had some land in this part of the country, and that I had come out to see about buying it. The old gentleman showed me the land, and stated he would be glad if his grandson would sell it and settle down with his father, near Brownwood.

Returning to Paris, I left at once for Brownwood, and upon arriving there, the deputy sheriff and I went to Mr. Hobart's, twenty miles from Brownwood. Mrs. Hobart informed me that her husband was two and a half miles from there, helping a neighbor kill hogs. When we arrived at this place, the deputy sheriff introduced me to someone as Jones, and just then a man stepped up and said, "Hello, Sullivan."

I had my mustache and beard blacked, in order to avoid detection by those who might know me; but this fellow seemed to recognize me after all.

"You must be mistaken in my name," I said, "for my name is Jones."

"You used to guard the jail in Mangum, in Greer County," he replied, "against a mob that wanted to hang Race Thomas and Jeff Adams for murder."

I told him he was mistaken in my name, and asked, "where is Mangum?"

"It is fifty-five miles north of Quanah, in Greer County," he replied.

"What road is Quanah on?" I asked.

"On the Fort Worth & Denver."

"I have never been any further north than Fort Worth," I replied.

He gave it up, and said he supposed he was mistaken. It was now dinner time, and we all went in and took our places around the table.

Tom Hobart, being a visitor, the host asked him to return thanks. He did so, and from the length of the blessing and the way he asked it, I imagined he was a Methodist. When he had finished, I said, "Gentlemen, we ought always to be thankful for the luxuries of life that we receive, but, as a general thing, we are not half as thankful as we should be."

"Are you a member of the church?" asked Hobart.

"Yes, sir, I am."

"To what church do you belong?"

"To the Methodist," I replied.

"Give me your hand;" he replied, "I am a Methodist too."

After dinner I told the old gentleman I had met his son and he told me about having some land on Emerson's prairie; that I had gone there and looked at the land, and was well pleased with it, and had about decided to quit renting land and buy me a place, and that I had come to Brown County to see about buying the land. He suggested that the deputy sheriff and I get in the buggy and go with him to the house and examine the papers. This we did. He got the deeds out of a trunk and handed them to me. I examined them very carefully, one by one. I could not have told whether they were right or wrong if my life had depended on it. I told him I couldn't see anything wrong with them. I asked where I could likely find his son, and he replied that he didn't know where he was, but that he would be glad for him to sell the place and settle down close to him, as he was a very wild boy.

This boy's father, Tom Hobart, was a commissioner and deputy sheriff of Brown County. After the deputy sheriff and I left the house, he turned to me and said:

"I have placed myself in a pretty shape by introducing you as Sam Jones to the old gentleman, for he will undoubtedly find out that this is all a fake about you buying land, and he will have it in for me.

"What kind of a man is he; is he a good man?"

"As good a man as ever lived," he replied.

"Suppose we go back and tell him the truth about the matter, and lay the case before him, and show him the letter written by his son to the boy's uncle, in which he confessed to the robbery? Do you think he would rather aid us in finding the boy than to have him still run at large, and probably be killed some day while robbing some bank or express car; or, if not killed, sent to the penitentiary for life?"

"I believe he would rather help us to find him," replied the deputy.

We concluded, therefore, to go back, and I told him my real name and why I was there. He turned pale and commenced trembling, and told me he thought there was something strange about the affair when I was talking to him about buying the land.

I explained to him what would probably be the fate of his son if he should run at large, and that I thought it would be better for him and better for the boy if his lawlessness should be checked.

The old gentleman agreed with me, and said that while he had no idea where the boy was at that time, he would aid me in every way in locating him.

I failed to find young Hobart, although I made every effort to do so. I have seen the deputy sheriff of Brown County several times, and he informs me that Tom Hobart has never heard of his boy from the time I was in Brown County looking for him.

Later on I caught Hobart's partner, Bill Hughes, thirty miles below Quanah; but, John Hobart being at large, Hughes could not be convicted.

XXXIV

BATTLE IN THE DUGOUT

I left Vernon on the 24th of December, 1896, with Sheriff Sanders, of Wilbarger County, and Bill Ish, to hunt for a train robber. We expected to locate him and another man, Tom Wright, whom we also wanted, at a dance that was to be given that night on Beaver Creek, twenty miles below Vernon. Wright was at the dance, as we had expected, but he made his escape before we got there.

After leaving the dance we went to an old gentleman's house, about two miles away, to spend the night, arriving there about half past one in the morning. We were quite hungry, as we had had no dinner or supper, so the lady brought out come cakes and pies, it being Chirstmas, and set them before us. They were delicious, and we ate a whole lot before we were through.

The next morning the family, which consisted of the man and his wife and their six grown children—three sons and three daughters—gathered together to have prayer. Of course we three men were there too. The old gentleman read a chapter of the Bible, and then called on Bill Ish to pray. Bill balked. He then called on Sheriff Sanders to pray, but the latter gentleman also failed to respond. I had already made up my mind that if he called on me, I was going to pray entirely for Bill and Dick (Sanders); but, for some reason, I was not called upon.

After spending a part of the day in that part of

GEORGE BLACK J. M. BRITTON

Two Ranger Boys of Company B. Britton was at one time Sergeant of the Company.

the country, we returned to Vernon, where I learned that there was a telegram for me at the depot. The message was from Taylor Holt, the book-keeper at Wagoner's store, and stated that four men had come to the store and beat one of the clerks nearly to death, and that they needed my assistance. I took Jack Harrell, a daring ranger, and we caught the train at once for Wagner.

When we arrived at Wagner, Taylor Holt was at the train to meet us, and took us over to the store, where he described the four desperadoes. When he expressed the opinion that the four men were still in the country, I said that we had better sleep in the store, as I thought the men would attempt to rob the store that night. There was a bed in the store, and, as I was tired, not having slept much in two days and nights, I lay down at once to go to sleep, after telling Holt to rouse me if he heard anyone and I was not the first to wake up.

About ten o'clock someone called at the front door of the store, and Holt and I awoke about the same time. Holt answered the call and told the party he was coming. I buckled on my sixshooter, picked up my Winchester, and went down the aisle in the store to where I struck the opening between two counters. I hid behind a show case and told Holt that when he got to the door to ask who it was, and, if he found it was the robbers, for him to drop flat on the floor behind the door after he opened it, and, as they stepped in, I would do the work for them. But when he asked who it was that they wanted, the party answered, "I am Alf Bailey; I was robbed awhile ago by four men."

We let him in, and Holt introduced us. Bailey said he was told that I was staying in Wagoner's store that night, and he had come to ask me to aid him in finding the robbers. Bailey's store was four miles south of Wagoner's store, and, instead of robbing Wagoner's store as we expected they would, the desperadoes robbed Alf Bailey's store and the postoffice, which was in the same building, getting about seven hundred dollars worth of merchandise and all the money and stamps in the postoffice.

Judging from Bailey's description of the men, I thought I knew one of them. I asked Holt if he had any horses we could use, and he replied that all of the horses were out in the pasture. It was about as cold a night, to be no wind blowing, as I ever saw in the Panhandle; so I told Bailey that as we had no horses it would be better for him to go back home and meet me in the morning with the trail. Bailey said he thought the four men went toward the Indian Territory.

I notified all the officers, up and down the line, of the robbery, so that they would be on the lookout for the robbers. I also wired the boys at headquarters to come down. The next morning Taylor Holt, Alf Bailey, and some others and I started out over the trail. The ground was frozen so hard that only one of the four horses made an impression on it, he weighing about twelve hundred pounds. After we had traveled some distance we came to a small house where the four men had spent the balance of the night. There were signs where they had fed the horses, and had cooked, eaten and slept. We also found a number of fine quirts between the mattresses, some tobacco, and about fifty pounds of còffee in a shed-room, which had been taken from Bailey's store. There was no one on the place but a big bull dog tied to the front door, and we had to enter the house through a window. Finding no one around anywhere, Taylor Holt and I went to the nearest house to see if we could get any information about the robbers. When we got to the house Holt went around to the back door while I knocked on the front door. I had to knock four or five times before I received an answer, and it was a lady who finally opened the door. About the same time I heard Holt speak to someone in the back yard. I hurried around there, and arrested a man who was just coming out of the back door. He was the owner of the house where the four desperadoes had stayed the night before. I asked him a few questions in regard to where he had stayed the night before, and who had stayed at his house, but I could get no information from him. I then asked him about the quirts, tobacco, and coffee at his house, and he said he knew nothing about them.

I thought it best to hold him for awhile, so Holt and I took him to the railroad, where we met a local. We hid our horses, boarded the local, went to Iowa Park, and met the north-bound passenger train. We then turned our prisoner over to an officer—Eugene Logan—with instructions to jail him at Vernon, and then we quit the train where we had left our horses. The night was so dark that we lost our way, and, after riding nearly all night, finally found ourselves at the house of a Mr. Cobbs, the place where I arrested the man the day before. Mr. Cobbs fed our horses for us, and I took time to sleep a little, after asking Mr. Cobbs to let us have breakfast as soon as they could get it ready, it then being about four o'clock in the morning.

After breakfast Mr. Cobbs told me that the man I arrested there the day before had taken his (Cobbs') hat and left his own new Stetson hat. I took possession of this new Stetson hat, and found that it had Mr. Bailey's cost-mark in it.

Holt and I then returned to Wagner, where we met the men whom we were with the day before. We also found there Sheriff Moses and Constable Tom Pickett, from Wichita Falls; Bud Hardin, a special ranger from Harrell; Dick Sanders, Sheriff of Wilbarger County; Johnnie Williams, Deputy Sheriff of Wilbarger County; Charley Landers, City Marshal of Vernon; Jack Harvell, Bob McClure, Billy McCauley, and Lee Queen, rangers, and Alf Bailey. I wired Sheriff Tittle, of Mangum, Greer County, fifty-five miles off the railroad, about the robbery.

My men and I left at once for Wagner's headquarters camp on Red River, where I got horses for the men, and where I received some information in regard to the four outlaws.

We traveled on toward the Indian Territory, and just before crossing Red River I met a man by the name of Dick Farrell, who was Tom Wagner's line camp rider, and who lived in the Indian Territory, twenty miles from Red River. I asked him if there was anyone at the line camp when he left, and he replied that there was no one there. I then asked him if he had seen anyone since he left the line camp, and he replied that he had seen two objects, but they were such a long distance off that he couldn't tell whether they were horses, cattle or men, and that he couldn't tell whether they were moving or standing still. He told me he had plenty to eat, and lots of horse feed at the camp, but had only one bed.

So we pushed on. About an hour before sundown, a big, blue norther blew up, which we had to face. Just at dusk we came in sight of Dick Farrell's camp, which was a dugout, half rock and half dirt, built in the head of a draw, and there was a bright light shining out of the mouth of the dugout down the draw. Six of my men had fallen behind; so I told the other five that those fellows in the dugout were either the outlaws or some hunters, and that we had better wait for the other men. We waited for some time, but they failed to come, and I told my men we would try it without the others. We started toward the dugout in a gallop, getting a little faster all the time, and when we got within seventy-five yards of the dugout, the four desperadoes—Joe Beckham, Hill Loftos, Redbuck, and the kid, Elmore Lewis—ran out and opened fire on us, killing three horses. I was making every effort to get my Winchester out of the scabbard, with all four of the outlaws shooting at us, but my horse was rearing and plunging so much to get away from the flare of the guns that every time I would reach down to pull my gun out, he would rear, and the horn of my saddle would knock me away from it; but, after three trials, and after getting a rib broken, I succeeded in getting my gun, when I fell off my horse and faced the four men. Three of them were in a trench leading into the dugout, and the fourth, Redbuck, was standing in the door of the dugout. I opened fire on them, as they were already shooting at us, and my first shot struck Redbuck just over the heart, and he fell backward into the dugout. The ball had only struck his breast-plate, however, and he fainted, but recovered in a few minutes and again joined in the fight. I found out afterward that we hit him again, shattering his collar bone and shoulder blade. I also learned that one of the men in the trench was killed. The firing was kept up until we had emptied our Winchesters and reloaded them. Suddenly I heard a gunshot behind me, and I turned and discovered that Johnnie Williams, the deputy sheriff of Wilbarger County, had come to my assistance. His horse had been killed in the fight, and Johnnie returned to me at once.

I asked Johnnie if he was hurt, and he replied that he was not, but added that I had better lie down on the ground or the desperadoes would kill me. Out of all the officers Johnnie was the stayer.

We fired several more shots at the three men, but they went into the dugout and fired at us from a window. I suggested to Johnnie that we dismount the four men by killing their horses, which we did, and every time we fired a horse fell. There were four animals in the pen, but it was so dark we couldn't see very well, and we afterward found that we had killed two of Wagner's horses, which they had stolen, and two of his big freight mules, which were used by Farrell. They had stolen two other horses from an old fellow in the Cheyenne country, but they had turned them out into the pasture. Later we captured these two horses and turned them over to their owner.

I suggested to Johnnie that we crawl across the draw and get in the corral, behind those dead horses, and kill the men as they came to the door. We then started crawling across the draw, keeping as close to the ground as we possibly could, when the men suddenly began firing on us again. Just at this time I fell over backward into a gully, and got fastened so tight that I had to make several efforts before I could get out. I was asking Johnnie all the time if he was hurt, and he crawled over to the edge of the gully that I was in and said he was not injured at all. I whispered to Johnnie that I had to get out of that gully, and if they killed me when I raised myself out of it, for him to shoot at the blaze and kill the man who shot me. I managed to get out of the gully, however, without being shot, and we began crawling again toward the corral, which was then about twenty steps away, and, if we could get behind the dead horses, we would only be about fifteen steps from the door of the dugout. We had gotten on high ground, when the three men "sky-lighted" us and opened fire again. Johnnie asked what we had better do, and I replied that it would not hurt to "crawfish" a little at that particular time, and we turned back, when we met three of the other men whom we left.

We fought the outlaws until eleven o'clock that night. Every time they saw any of us moving anywhere they fired at us, and we fired back at them. Finally, we got so cold we couldn't pull a cartridge from our belts, and couldn't work the lever of our Winchesters, and we had to quit. We decided to go back that night to Wagner's camp, which was twenty-five miles away; so we started out, walking across the country.

We arrived at Wagner's camp the next morning, and I gave Dick Farrell five dollars to guide me back across the country to the dugout. All of my men, except Billy McCauley and Lee Queen, refused to go back with me; so with these two men and Dick Farrell, I left for the dugout in a blinding storm of snow and sleet. When we arrived at Red River, Dick Farrell decided that he didn't care to go to the dugout if we went together, for if the men were still there they would open fire on us as they did the night before. He suggested that he go alone, and, if they were there, to tell them he was the owner of the dugout, and that he would report to me that night. I concluded to let him do this. Farrell then went to the dugout, and my men and I returned to Wagner's ranch. That evening Farrell returned to the ranch, and stated that the desperadoes had left the dugout, but he found Sheriff Tittle, of Greer County, there, with John Byers and Jim Farris, two of his deputies. Tittle told Farrell there had been a fight there the night before, and one man killed, and he asked Farrell if he knew who had been in the fight. Farrell told him it was Sullivan and his officers and the four outlaws. He then instructed Farrell to return to Wagner's ranch, and tell me that he and his men had come to the dugout to investigate the matter, and that Joe Beckham, ex-sheriff of Motley County, had been killed the night before, and that there had been seven horses killed, and for me to come there at once, and he would stay until I arrived.

Farrell returned to me with this information, and I immediately got a buckboard and a pair of mules from Tom Wagner, and, with Alf Bailey, Billy McCauley and Lee Queen, went to the dugout, where I found Sheriff Tittle and his two men. Before we entered the dugout, where Alf Bailey's goods were, we had him tell us his cost-mark. We examined the goods, the cost-mark on them tallied with the cost-mark Bailey had given us before seeing the goods, and we recovered nearly all of the merchandise that had been stolen from Bailey.

I put Beckham's body in the buckboard, and then loaded in seven saddles, three of which we took off the dead horses, and four which belonged to the four outlaws. I also put in Alf Bailey's goods, and then returned to Wagner's station on the Fort Worth & Denver Railroad. The next day, Tuesday, we buried Beckham, but the following Thursday I received orders from Adjutant General Mabry to hold an inquest over Beckham's body, and we had to take the body up and hold an inquest over it that day. Before burying him again, however, I took his wife's ring off his finger.

Beckham had a sister living in Altis, and one night while I was in that town she sent for me to ask me about her brother. I went to see her and gave her the ring which I had taken from her brother's finger. I explained to her the manner in which her brother had met his death, and, although terribly grieved, she said she could not hold me responsible for his sad fate. She said her brother had once been an honorable man, but had gradually gotten bad, and kept getting worse, until his untimely and tragic end was inevitable.

XXXV

AN EXCITING EXPERIENCE WITH INDIANS

After the battle in the dugout, I returned to Amarillo, and nine days later I received a message from the operator at Wagner, and one from Taylor Holt also, saying that there was a man in Paint Creek dugout by the name of Redbuck, and that he was very badly wounded and expected to die, and that his friends were making arrangements to carry him further off.

At that time all of my ranger boys were out on a scouting expedition; so I sent to Vernon for the deputy marshal, and wired C. Madson, of El Reno, chief of the marshals, to send me one of his deputies, and he sent me Ed Meyers. I also had Jailer Shics of Vernon; Tom Pickett, constable of Wichita Falls; Sam Abbott, of Wichita Falls; Charley Landers, city marshal of Vernon, and Henry McCauley, of Wichita Falls.

With these men I went to S. B. Burnett's headquarters camp, ten miles from Wichita Falls, where I succeeded in getting a wagon and a span of mules, and horses for myself and men, and plenty of bacon, beef, coffee, flour and horse feed.

We then started out, with Henry McCauley as teamster. That night we camped at Burnett's line camp in the Territory. Before we reached this place, however, we had quite a lively scene. There were two negroes and an old white man at the line camp. They saw us when we were seaeral hundred yards away, and thought we were outlaws, and the two negroes, one with a six-shooter and the other with a Winchester, were trying to get to a thicket about two hundred yards from the camp. The old white man was standing on the gallery trying to get the negroes to stay there, and he finally succeeded, after they had jumped the fence three or four times. When we reached the camp, the two negroes, Zip and Jack, told us they thought we were Foster Crawford's gang. The white man had taken out a little note-book before we reached the camp, and had written in it, "I was killed by outlaws." I told him he made his will too quick. Zip was scared so badly that his face was a creamy color, although he was naturally as black as the ace of spades. I asked him if he had been powdering his face, as it looked nearly white, and he replied that he was so badly frightened that he didn't know whether his face would ever resume its original color or not. Things quieted down, and old Zip, being also badly scared, cooked us a fine supper that night.

As I was not very well acquainted with that section of the country, the next morning I concluded it would be better to have some one to go with us who was familiar with the country; so I got Jack to go in front of us, and I told him that whenever he came near a dugout he must go ahead and see if everything was all right, and then report to me, as I did not want to rush myself and the boys into anything without first knowing a few particulars.

Jack located several dugouts, and came back and reported each time that there were no strangers or wounded men in any of them. About eleven o'clock that day, Jack had gotten careless and had fallen behind with the teamster. Ed Meyers and I were riding in the lead. While looking ahead of us I saw a little box house about eight hundred yards away, and a moment later I beheld three people running out of it, two at the back of the house and one in the front. I motioned to the men to come on, and Jack ran his horse up beside me, and I asked him who lived in the house. He replied that a family of white people lived there. We ran our horses toward the house, and, after we had run about five hundred yards, Jack said he saw a buggy leave the house; but as neither Meyers nor I had seen this buggy, we rode straight for the house, while Jack kept leaning to the left, away from the house. Meyers and I ran up to the back of the house, and there we found a buggy, but there was no team hitched to it. I remarked to Meyers, "Look where Jack is; he sees something," and we ran our horses toward Jack. After we had gone about five hundred yards we discovered this buggy coming around a hill, and they were riding around to get on our left; so I told Meyers to kill their horses, as he was riding next to them and my Winchester was a long one and hard to handle on horseback. After Meyers fired, they began firing on us, and I told him to quit shooting and wait until they started down a string of wire fence, and we would then follow them. "When we get close enough to them, I will get off my horse and tear the back out of the buggy," I said. Just as I was about to dismount Jack threw his hat in the air and yelled "Comanches!" We then saw an Indian, whose name I afterward learned was "Crowmore," come out of Oak Creek, riding a Paint pony, and he fired two shots at us with his Winchester, yelling "sheepshicr," meaning "hurry up." About this time we discovered that the people in the buggy whom we were after were Indians, three of whom were Crowmore's wife, and papoose, and his brothre-in-law. Crowmore and the other three Indians in the buggy then went down to their camp.

Jailer Shies proposed going to the camp and explaining things, as he was acquainted with Crowmore, but I advised him to stay away, as Crowmore would not know him from any other officer if he saw him riding up to his camp, and, as he was on the warpath, he might shoot him. Shies insisted, however, and I told him if he would go that he had better go alone; for, if several of us went, Crowmore would likely fire on us before we could get him located.

Shies decided to go alone, and after he had been gone some time I began to feel uneasy about him; so I took Sam Abbott, Ed Meyers and Jack and went down to the camp to see what the trouble was. I found no one there, but while searching for Shies, I found a rope stretched in the yard loaded with what I took to be beef. I dismounted and ate a big lot of Crowmore's nice beef, and then got my men and went back to the little house which we had left sometime before. There I found the other members of my party, and they were just getting ready for dinner.

I told them that I had eaten so much good beef that I was not hungry and did not want any dinner.

"Where did you get the beef?" the lady of the house asked me.

"Down at Crowmore's camp," I replied.

"That beef you ate down there was an old horse that died a few day ago, and they 'jerked' him on that rope," she said.

"Well, he was 'jerked' twice then if they jerked him, for I 'jerked' him once myself," I answered. I did not say anything else, but my meat didn't set very well after that.

About fifteen minutes after I arrived at this house, and while watching for Shies, I saw forty-six Indians riding toward the house as fast as their horses could carry them. When the lady, who lived at the house where we were, saw them, she said that they were on the warpath; for she had lived in that section of the country fifteen years and knew their ways. The Indians came within five hundred yards of where we were, and, with their horses, formed a figure eight. Jack said that was a sign that they were going to fight us, and when they made three such figures it meant they were coming. They went back a short distance, and then came toward us and made another figure eight, leaving them one more to make before they charged us. I then discovered two Indians running their horses toward the hay stacks, back of the house. I saw at once that if they reached the hay stacks, they would have the advantage of us; so I sent Charley Landers and Sam Abbott to head them off, and, after a quick chase, they beat the Indians to the stacks, and the Indians returned and joined the others, who were getting ready to make the third figure eight.

This lady, whom I have spoken of several times, informed me that she could speak the Indian language as well as they could, and offered to go to the Indians and deliver any message I might wish to send them. I accepted her proposition, and asked her to tell them that we were Texas rangers and we had a deputy marshal from El Reno with us; that we had come to this house to look for a wounded man by the name of Redbuck; that we heard they were going to take him away in a buggy; that when we saw the buggy leave the house so hurriedly we concluded the man we wanted was in the buggy, and consequently had tried to kill the horses which were hitched to the buggy, not knowing we were after Crowmore's people.

After I explained to the lady what to tell the Indians, she started toward them, swinging her blue bonnet in the air to let them know she wished to speak to them. She explained the situation to them, but they told her we had deceived her, and also told her they knew we were outlaws, as they had been informed at Fort Sill that the country was full of them, and that there had been a fight about twenty-five miles below there a few nights back, and they were satisfied we had come to kill their people.

She returned and reported what they had told her. I then asked her to go to them and state to them that Tom Pickett, constable from Wichita Falls, was with our men, and that they ought to know him, as he had managed their war dances for them at Wichita Falls, and that he could prove to them that we were officers.

She did this, and informed us that the Indians said to send Tom Pickett to them. Tom didn't seem to be very anxious to make the visit to the

"SKEETER"
One of Bill Cook's favorite warriors. Today in Sing Sing, N. Y., serving his thirty years' sentence.

Indians just then, but I told him to lay his Winchester down on the ground where they could see it, and to go to them and try to make a treaty with them, and that if they killed him, I would kill every one of them before they could get back to Fort Sill. Tom concluded to go, and Henry McCauley, the teamster, volunteered to go with him. When they reached the Indians they recognized Tom at once, and the chief dismounted and took Tom and Henry by the hands, and seemed to be very glad to find out that we were not outlaws.

He instructed his warriors to stay where they were, while he investigated the matter a little more. He mounted his horse and came toward us at full speed, and when he arrived within seventy yards of us, he threw his Winchester across his left wrist. This was a sign that we were friends, but I didn't know it at the time, and I came very near shooting him, but Jack stopped me and explained what was meant by it.

When he reached us, he dismounted, shook hands with us all, and then motioned for his men to come, and they, with Tom and Henry, soon joined us.

I cautioned the men not to let the Indians get to our guns, and not to be too free with them. The Indians would point to our belts and indicate to us that they wanted us to give them some cartridges, which we did.

The chief informed me that Crowmore's wife had gone to Fort Sill, where she would report that we were outlaws, and that the police and soldiers would be looking for us in a short while, and we had better hire two of his men to stay with us the balance of that day and that night, in order to assist us in explaining our presence in the country, and that if I would give him five dollars he would let me have two of his men. I told him I would give him two dollars and a half, but he would not consent to take less than five dollars; so we agreed upon that amount. All this conversation was carried on, of course, with the help of the lady who was with us.

When I first saw that the Indians were convinced that we were not outlaws, I told the lady to ask them if they had seen anything of a white man; for I was uneasy about Shies, not having seen him since he went to Crowmore's camp; but the Indians replied that they had not seen anyone at all. A few minutes later Shies rode up, and said that he had just been riding around the country scouting.

XXXVI

THE ARREST OF JEROME LOFTOS

While in Vernon helping to hold court in the trial of Joe Blake, who was alleged to have killed Sheriff Tom McGee, in Hemphill County, I received a warrant from Bowie County for the arrest of Jerome Loftos, who was wanted for stabbing a man in New Boston ten years before that.

I did not know that Loftos was in Vernon until Mrs. Aiken, the proprietress of the hotel, told me that a man by the name of Jerome Loftos was in the hotel the night before to see me. I asked Mrs. Aiken when the man would be back, and she replied, "In a day or two."

I told Mrs. Aiken that I would be glad to see Jerome, as I had not seen him but once, and that was a few days after the fight which I had had with his brother, Hill Loftos, in the dugout in the Comanche Strip. I began watching for Loftos, and the second morning after the lady told me that he was in town, I went into the gentlemen's sitting-room and found him standing by the stove. I did not recognize him, however, until after he had spoken to me and told me his name.

When he told me that he was Jerome Loftos, I merely asked him if he had eaten his breakfast, and he replied that he had not.

The first table was full, so I told him that we would watch our chance and eat at the next table.

When we went to the table I let him sit on my right side, and I made it a point to get through eating before he did. Leaving the table after breakfast, we went into the gentlemen's sitting-room, where I found about twenty-five men standing around. I did not want to arrest Loftos in the presence of these people, and, noticing that the stove in the ladies' sitting-room was heated up, I said to Loftos, "Let's go in yonder where there is a good fire."

After we got in the room I told Loftos that I had a warrant for him.

"Where from?" he asked.

"From New Boston," I replied.

I searched him then, but found nothing but a pocket knife. I told him that I did not want to handcuff him, nor put him in jail; that for his sake I didn't want people to know that he was under arrest.

I then notified the sheriff of New Boston that I had his man, but it was three days before he came to Vernon after him. I never jailed Loftos, though, nor put handcuffs on him, but I kept him in my sight all the time. I told Loftos to go with me when I took Joe Blake to the trial, and for him to sit near Blake, the defendant, so I could watch both of them at the same time.

When the sheriff came after him, I told him that Loftos had behaved well, and that he deserved the good treatment which he had received at my hands. I told the sheriff that I would appreciate it if he would also treat him as courteously as the circumstances justified, as Loftos had been a good citizen ever since he stabbed the man ten years before, and that he had been a good prisoner.

Just as the train was pulling in Loftos asked me

to let him speak to me. We walked a few steps away from the sheriff, and I told him that I was ready to listen to him.

He asked me if I knew what he thought of me, and I told him that I did not.

"I think you have been giving me dirt ever since you arrested me," he replied.

I immediately turned Loftos over to the sheriff, telling the latter that he had better handcuff and shackle him securely, as I had learned that I was greatly deceived in the prisoner, when I recommended him so highly a few minutes before. I told Loftos that I was mighty glad he let me know what he thought of me before it was too late for me to do him any service. The sheriff did as I told him, and securely shackled and handcuffed Loftos, much to the latter's displeasure.

Loftos stood his trial in New Boston and came clear. A year later I met him on a Fort Worth & Denver train, while I was going to Fort Worth. I was talking to a lady, when Loftos came through the car and greeted me, and told me that he wanted to see me in the smoker. I told him "alright." He then turned and went back into the smoker.

"Who is that gentleman?" the lady asked.

I told her that he was Jerome Loftos, and that I had once arrested him in Vernon. I also told her what Loftos said to me when the train rolled into Quanah, and, I added, that he might want to call my hand for telling the sheriff to handcuff and shackle him.

"You ought not to go into the smoker if you think there will be trouble," she replied.

I told her that I would go anyway, but when I

entered the smoking car, Loftos got up and introduced me to four or five men and treated me as cordially as he knew how. He motioned me to a vacant seat, and later on apologized to me for what he had said to me before he boarded the train in Quanah. "You treated me so nice when you had me in your charge," he said, "that I have been sorry ever since then that I told you that you had been giving me dirt; for I knew at the time that you had not."

"What prompted you to make such a remark, then?" I asked.

"I was mad at the world in general," he replied, "for I had led a better life ever since I cut the man in New Boston, and had worked hard on the ranches, and had saved my earnings and accumulated a little bunch of cattle. I had gotten a little start in life, and felt happy; but when you arrested me I realized that it was 'all up' with me then, and knew I would have to spend everything I had to come clear. I was reckless, and never thought about what I said to you, but I am ashamed of it now, and hope you will forgive me and forget that incident."

I told him that I had already forgiven him, and we were good friends ever after.

XXXVII

THE CAPTURE AND TRIAL OF SWIN

In 1896 the citizens around Amarillo were constantly losing their fat cattle, and could not locate the cause, and I was informed by John Curry, who lived in the north edge of town, that he suspected old man Crump and his two sons, Albert and Bill, who lived two miles north of town, who were running a butcher shop in Amarillo. Albert Crump lived in town, and did the selling of the beef. After learning all this from John Curry, I decided to lie around Crump's place, and try to catch him and his two boys in case they were stealing cattle. I watched the old man's place for quite awhile.

One evening Sam Dunn and Hank Siders (both cattle inspectors) and I waylaid Crump's pasture, and a little before dark we heard a gunshot at his slaughter house. We waited about half an hour, in order to give him time to get his beef skinned, but we stayed a little too long. Billy, his son, about twenty-two years of age, took the beef to the city and placed it in the butcher shop. I followed the hack, and got there in time to stand out in the dark and see Billy carve the beef. The quarters of this beef looked to me, from a distance, to be about a two or three-year-old animal. I could see them from the light he had in his butcher shop. I said nothing to Bill; not even letting him know that I was in town.

Hank and Sam and I went back to old man Crump's. It must have been about ten o'clock at night. I called out at the gate, and learned that old man Crump had gone to bed. He got up, however, and came about half way from the house to the gate, and asked me who I was.

I told him that it was Sullivan.

He told me to wait a minute until he went into the house to put on his shoes, as he was barefooted. I waited, although I believed that he was trying to "make medicine" or work his rabbit foot on me. When he got to the door I saw his wife slipping out to the west gate, in a stooped position, making her way to the slaughter house. I told her to come back, and not go about the slaughter house. She obeyed my command.

Then I asked the old man if he had killed a beef that evening.

He said that he had.

I told him that I wanted to see the hide.

He said that it was in the slaughter house.

We three dismounted and went to the slaughter house, and came very nearly being taken in by the worst set of dogs I ever saw. He must have had eight or ten vicious dogs. I think he kept those dogs on hand to bluff people, so they would not come anywhere about his place.

When we arrived at the slaughter house, he pulled a hide out of a barrel of brine and threw it on the floor, with the hair side up. It being wet, it rattled as if it were a green hide. This hide must have been seven or eight days old. It was so dark in the slaughter house that I could not tell whether this was a fresh hide or an old one. I rubbed my hand over the hide and got the scent of it, and told the boys that the hide was an old one. I struck a match, and, as the slaughter house was open at the top, the wind would blow my matches out as fast as I could strike them. At last I told Mrs. Crump to go into the house and bring me a lamp or a lantern. She remarked that the wind would blow the lamp or lantern, either one, out, and that we had better take the hide into the house; so I told the old man to take hold of one end of the hide and Hank the other. When we got into the house and threw the hide on the floor, I discovered that it was black, and that it was an old one with a brand on it,

The old man asked me to let him step out of doors. I granted him this privilege, knowing that he was going to the slaughter house. The old man went directly to the slaughter house, and I went directly to the same place. When I reached the place I heard him drop the hide in this barrel of brine. Then he picked up a zinc tub to put over the barrel, and, as he did so, I arrested him.

We left at once for town. After turning him over to Hank and Sam, I went to meet Billy, to arrest him and to keep him away from his father, so they could not "make medicine" together.

I arrested Billy, and asked him a few questions in regard to the killing of this beef. I asked him if he had a bill of sale for the beef.

He stated that he had.

I asked him the name of the party he got the beef from, but he said he could not remember the name, still claiming that he had a bill of sale for the beef.

I talked with him until his father was within hearing distance of him, and he called out something to Billy in German, and I told Billy to turn his wagon around, and I took him to town and turned him over to John Bell, telling the latter to hold Billy until I arrested his brother, Albert, who was asleep in the butcher shop.

As soon as I arrested Albert he asked where "Pa and Billy" were. I told him that I had them under arrest, too. "Lord, have mercy," was all he had to say.

I placed the old gentleman in jail, and took Billy and Albert to my camp and shackled Billy to one of the ranger boys and Albert to another one, not letting either one of them speak to their father, nor to each other.

The case was called for trial in Amarillo, but the defense got a change of venue to Clarendon, Donley County, and Billy was convicted, but got a new trial, and finally beat his case. The old man and Albert were also acquitted in their trial at Clarendon. John Veale and Bill Plemmans, two attorneys from Amarillo, defended them.

Mrs. Crump had three small children. Judge Plemmans and Judge Veale were shrewd enough to borrow three more children who lived in Clarendon, keeping the six children around Mrs. Crump all the time the trial was going on. In their speeches, the attorneys for the defense, would refer to the old lady and her six small children, keeping the old lady constantly crying and rubbing her hand over the six children's heads. When she and her six children would cease crying, Judge Plemmans would step over to the woman and tell her that if she didn't keep the children and herself crying that the old man and the two boys would go to the pen "as sure as God made little apples." Once the old lady spoke out loud, and said that she had already cried so much that she couldn't cry any more if the whole family went to the pen. This caused quite a laugh in the court room at the expense of Messrs. Veale and Plemmans.

XXXVIII

THE CAPTURE OF IHART AND SPREY

While at headquarters camp at Amarillo in 1896, I received a letter from Jim Loving, President of the Cattlemen's Association, asking me to go to San Angelo and out to Big Lake, in Tom Green County, and look through Major Look and his brother's pasture for burnt cattle. I went to San Angelo at once, and hired a wagon and team, and got Sheriff Shields and Cattle Inspector Moore to go out to Big Lake with me. I also took two negroes along, one to drive and cook, and the other to rustle the horses.

While on my way to Big Lake, which is one hundred and five miles from San Angelo, I drew on my imagination considerably as to the kind of a lake I was going to and the scenery around it. I thought the lake would be full of good, clear water, and that I would see lots of antelope, deer, wild cats, coyote and lobo wolves, going there late in the evening for water. The lake was a mile and a half long and half a mile wide.

We reached the lake at sunset, and our horses were very tired and thirsty, and so were we, but we didn't find a drop of water in that lake, and had to drive until late in the night before we could find water.

Early the next morning we went to Look's pasture, where we spent the three following days rounding up the cattle and looking for burnt brands. We expected to find about a hundred burnt cattle, but only found three. We took them to San Angelo and gave them back to their owners. Then we arrested Major Look and his brother, and turned them over to the sheriff, and they were reported to the grand jury.

The day after I had arrested the two Look brothers, a man walked up to me on the street and asked me if I was an officer, and I replied that I was.

"Do you see that man standing on the sidewalk, about twenty steps from me on my left?" he then asked.

I replied that I did.

"I want you to arrest him," he said.

"What for?" I asked.

"He stole a five-dollar pair of pants from me at the hotel the other night, and he has them on now," he answered.

I asked him if he would swear to the pants.

"If I could get to examine them, I would," he replied.

I arrested the man and took him to the rear of a nearby store, and the man who made the complaint went with us, and after examining the pants he swore that they were his. I then searched my prisoner, and found on him a pistol and some letters. Reading one of the letters, which was from his best girl in the Nation, I gained some valuable information concerning this man's record. A portion of the letter read this way:

"Pet, you have treated your baby bad by stealing those horses and that saddle. The officers are hot on your trail, but my people are trying to make them believe that you are in Kansas and not in

Texas. You have gone to a mighty good place to get caught, Pet, and you had better get out of that State or you will be taken in. I am perfectly surprised at you, Pet, for committing that crime, and I don't see how you could have done it if you loved me."

I learned that this man was Jack Ihart, a noted highway robber and horse thief. I turned him over to the sheriff, and he notified the officers in the Nation, and they immediately came after him, as he was very much wanted up there. Carrying sweethearts' letters got him into a lot of trouble.

The following night a man asked me if I wasn't Sullivan, the ranger, and I told him that I was.

"My name is Ed Smith. I guess you have heard of me before," he said. "I am an ex-convict, but I have something important to tell you."

I told him "all right," and he asked me if I wanted a man by the name of Hill Loftos.

I told him that I did, and that I wanted him very badly.

He asked me if there was a reward out for him, and I told him that there was.

Then he told me that if I would give him half the reward he would point Hill Loftos out to me.

I told him that I would do that.

He then told me that Hill Loftos was in the back end of a saloon gambling. I went to the hotel and got my handcuffs and put them in my pocket. Then we went to the saloon which he claimed Loftos was in. Reaching the front door, I told Smith to go in and see if Loftos was still playing cards. He came back and reported that Loftos was not in there. We then went to every saloon in town, and I sent Smith into all of them to see if he could find Loftos, but he always reported that he failed to find him.

Smith then said that Loftos had two aunts living near the depot, on the edge of the town, and that he might have gone to their house to go to sleep; so we struck out in that direction to find our man. It occurred to me that Smith might be leading me into a trap, as the house where the two old maids lived was surrounded by timber, and there were no lights in that part of the town; so I kept a close eye on the man who was helping me to find Hill Loftos.

After reaching the depot, we inquired at ten or twelve houses to find out where the two old maid sisters lived, and were beginning to think that we would not succeed in locating the house, when we finally came to a house where the yard was full of pretty shade trees. The front gate was tied at the bottom with wire; so we went around to the back gate and found it, also, tied so it couldn't be opened. Thinking this place was vacant, we went across the street and aroused a lady, who told us that the two old maids lived in the house where the yard was full of trees, which was the place where we had tried to open the gate.

I told Ed to go in the house and see if Hill Loftos was there. "If you see him," I said, "you tell him that you have won a big piece of money at a gambling dive; that a big game is going on, and that you are willing to stake him with money, and both go in together and see if you can't win a hundred dollars." I told Smith that I would hide at the corner of the paled fence, and that I would watch the gate and when he came out I would join them. I gave him instructions to stop and roll a cigarette when he came out, so that I would have plenty of time to catch up with him.

Smith carried out my instructions to the letter. When I came out, I caught up with them and said, "Hello, gentlemen." Both of them spoke very cordially to me. It was about one o'clock in the morning.

I remarked that I had started down town to get a drink of beer, and asked them where the nearest saloon was. They pointed one out that was about forty yards in front of us. I invited them to take a glass of beer with me, and they said they would "with pleasure," and we went on toward the saloon.

While walking along I let Hill Loftos get a yard ahead of me, and I eased my sixshooter from the scabbard, holding on the trigger all the time, so it would not click when I cocked it.

When I got everything in shape, I stepped up to his side and threw my sixshooter cocked in his face, and ordered, "hands up." He at once threw his left hand above his head, but placed his right hand over his heart. "Both hands up," I quickly said, and he immediately put his right hand up. I then pulled my handcuffs out, and, giving them to Ed, I told him to put them on Loftos, which he did. Then I arrested Ed, too, and asked him his name. He said it was Ed Smith. I did not want Ed, but did this to keep Loftos from thinking that Ed had told on him.

Turning to the other man, I asked if he wasn't Hill Loftos, and he said he was not; that "Jack

Sprey" was his name. He said he was from Greer County.

"Have you been passing yourself off as Hill Loftos?" I asked.

"No; I have not."

I told him that I would hold him, anyway, and I carried him over and placed him in jail. I told Ed, in Sprey's presence, that I would guard them both, but, when daylight came, I turned Ed loose, of course; but I took the other man to Vernon, where I learned that he was wanted in the Indian Territory for horse theft. This man really was not Hill Loftos, but he told Ed that was his name, because he knew of Loftos' bad reputation as a fighter, and he wanted Ed to be afraid of him. Hill Loftos is the man with whom I had such a fight in the dugout in the Comanche Strip, twenty-five miles from Fort Sill.

XXXIX

A PRIZE FIGHT PREVENTED

While I was stationed at Amarillo, in 1896, our entire company, and three other companies, were ordered by Governor Culberson to go to El Paso, to keep the Fitzsimmons-Maher fight from being fought in Texas.

We stayed in El Paso eighteen days to see that these prize fighters didn't pull off their exhibition in Texas.

We, also, had to put down the tough element of the town, as thieves, robbers, pickpockets, and other classes of criminals were giving a great deal of trouble.

One night while City Marshal John Sulman and I were on duty, we arrested twenty-six burglars and jailed them, one making his escape. John Sulman is the man who killed John Welsey Hardin in an El Paso saloon.

One night, while in that saloon where Hardin was killed, I met John L. Sullivan and Paddy Ryan, prize fighters. While Sullivan and I were trying to rake up relationship, I noticed that Ryan's nose had been broken, and I asked him what caused it.

"Fourteen years ago," he replied, "Sullivan and I had a prize fight in Mississippi and he warped my nose."

About that time I heard a lot of shooting on the street. Sullivan, Ryan, and I were in the back of the building, and about three hundred men, the largest portion of whom were full of beer and whiskey, stood between me and the front door.

When I heard the shooting, I was satisfied that some of the ranger boys had gotten into trouble with some tough character, and I decided to go to the street as quickly as I could and see what was the matter. I finally pulled through this crowd of men and reached the door, and when I stepped out upon the street, I heard three more shots. I located the direction of the shooting from the flash of the pistols, and discovered it was a special ranger trying to arrest an El Paso gambler, and a deputy sheriff from Greenville, who had fallen out over a game of cards and had come out upon the street to settle their trouble. When the two men reached the street, the ranger told them to be quiet or he would arrest them. The gambler got mad and fired at the ranger, and a general shooting scrape followed. Though each man fired several shots, no one was hurt.

We arrested the two men who had resisted the ranger, and took them into the saloon through the back entrance. Much excitement prevailed among the men in the saloon, but after placing the two prisoners in the keeping of other officers, I went out the back way and walked around the building to guard the front door, as a crowd of men were trying to break it down and get into the saloon.

I had ordered the door shut when the shooting first occurred, because I did not want anybody else to get into the building. There were about four hundred men, all tough characters, standing in the street with their sixshooters out, shining like new money. They tried a number of times to make me let them in, but I held the door shut against them. I knew that most of them were robbers and cut-throats, and that if they got into that crowd of men in the saloon they would spot out the diamonds and watches and shoot the lights out, and great slaughter and robbery would come off.

Gen. W. H. Mabry, our State Adjutant General, came to me and told me to put my pistol up.

I told him that I could not do it. About that time Eugene Miller, a special ranger, who was helping me to hold the door, yelled at me to "look out." I glanced quickly around, and there, standing behind me, was the man who stole Bill Cook away from me in Roswell, N. M. I could see the handle of his sixshooter, which he held in his hand behind him.

Recognizing the man, in a moment, I turned and asked Miller why he had called me in such an exciting manner.

"Everything is all right now," replied Miller, and the man left before anything else was said about the incident.

In a few minutes, however, Miller asked me if I knew who that tall man was, who stood at my back, when he called to me to "look out."

I told him that I did; that it was the man who stole Bill Cook from me, and with whom I had had some trouble as the result.

Miller then told me that the man had his pistol cocked and pointed at my spine, and that when he called out to me, the man threw his hand and pistol behind him.

It seems that the man was about to take advantage of the moment, while confusion reigned, and murder me from behind, because of his grudge against me. I told Miller that if I had caught the man pointing his gun at me, I would have killed him on the spot.

I can safely say that I saw more tough characters in El Paso at that time than I ever saw before in my life, or ever expect to see again. They were drawn to that town by the prize fight, which was about to be pulled off there. It took one hundred and fifty officers to preserve order and prevent the prize fight.

The fight was pulled off in Old Mexico, about four hundred miles down the Rio Grande River. I wanted to go and see the fight, but I was requested by the Adjutant General to remain in El Paso with eleven rangers and help guard the three banks, which I did.

XL

A BANK ROBBERY

We went to El Paso in November, 1896, with four companies of rangers to prevent the prize fight between Fitzsimmons and Maher. After staying there about eighteen days, I started back to headquarters. Two of my men asked me to let them get off at Bowie for a day, and I consented, after instructing them to come to Amarillo the next day, as we would likely have a great deal of work to do. I continued on my way to Amarillo, and when I reached Wichita Falls I received a telegram from C. Madson, the Chief Marshal at El Reno, I. T., to come there and surrender to him as I had a fight in the Comanche Strip. Two of my boys, Jack Howell and Lee Queen, were on the train with me, and I told them to get off and go to El Reno with me. They requested me, however, to let them go on to headquarters and get some clothes, and they come on to El Reno on the following day. This was agreeable to me; so I spent that night in Wichita Falls, and the boys joined me next day, and we started to El Reno, after wiring to the other two men, who were on the north-bound train, coming from Bowie, to join me.

When I arrived at Bellview I received a telegram to return to Wichita Falls on the north-bound train, as Frank Dorsey, the cashier of the bank at that place, had been killed and four men wounded by robbers. My two men and I then boarded the north-bound train, where I found my other two men, who had stopped at Bowie. Captain Bill McDonald also was on the north-bound train.

Mr. J. A. Kemp, the president of the bank that was robbed at Wichita Falls, was on the south-bound train, and I told him to return to Wichita Falls with me, as he was needed at his bank. I stepped into the office and asked Annanias Moore, the operator, to wire the operator at Wichita Falls, to have me six horses and saddles waiting at the depot when I arrived at Wichita Falls. I asked George Clark, the conductor on the train, to put me in Wichita Falls before schedule time; but I think, from the rate the train ran, we reached Wichita Falls a little ahead of time.

Mr. Kemp sat down by me, and asked me what the trouble was. I told him that his bank had been robbed, his cashier, Frank Dorsey, had been killed, and four other men had been wounded. He turned pale, and tears came into his eyes as he said, "Frank came to me this morning and asked me to let him resign, as he had a presentiment that he was going to be killed, but I talked him out of it."

Three months before Dorsey was killed, I was called to Wichita Falls to guard the two banks, as twelve suspicious looking characters had been seen camping out near town, and the citizens thought they were bank robbers. I took six rangers with me, and we guarded the two banks for three days and nights. We went out one evening to the place where the men had camped, and found pictures of Bill Cook, Jim French, Frank Baldwin, Cherokee Bill, and other noted outlaws, thus confirming the suspicions of the citizens who were uneasy about the banks.

While we were guarding the banks on that occasion, Frank Dorsey came to me several times and said that he feared that he would be killed, but I told him there was no danger, as my men could hold out against any robbers. The suspicious characters left the country after we began guarding the banks, and the citizens of Wichita Falls no longer felt uneasy; so we rangers packed up and went back to Amarillo.

Three months passed away, and everything was quiet and peaceful in Wichita Falls until the dreadful day of the bank robbery, when the cashier, Frank Dorsey, was killed. The night before the robbery, Dorsey told his wife that the presentiment that he would be killed by bank robbers had come back to him stronger than ever. He said that he would resign his position the next morning; that he believed that if he didn't, he would be killed in a short time.

His wife told him that it was all imagination; that he ought not to give up his work, as he had a family to support, and the president of the bank thought so much of him. He was easily persuaded by those arguments not to resign, and the next evening his dead body was carried home to a heartbroken wife, and the president of the bank was on the train hurrying back to Wichita Falls, mourning the loss of a fine cashier and valuable friend.

When we arrived at Wichita Falls, my horses were standing at the depot; but just as I stepped off the train, twenty or thirty men rushed me into the depot, telling me that the bank had been robbed and Frank Dorsey killed by two men, and they could talk of nothing else but the reward—two thousand dollars—which had been offered by the bankers for the capture of the robbers. I told them not to talk to me about rewards, but to give me the descriptions of the two men. They did so, and we started out after them. Some of the citizens of the town were already out after the two robbers, but after we had gone a short distance, we met most of them coming back to town. Some of them, however, turned and joined us in our pursuit.

It was related to us that as the two robbers, whose names I learned to be Elmer Lewis and Foster Crawford, started out of town, Frank Hogister killed Lewis' horse, and he rode behind Crawford until they met a man driving a little dun mare. They relieved this man of his animal, which Elmer rode bareback. They soon met two men, who were plowing in the river bottom, and took their two large plow horses, releasing the ones they were riding. These two plow horses were so large, though, that they didn't last long, and we soon found where the robbers had tied them in a thicket and then waded the Wichita River.

Some of the men went a mile below this place and crossed the river on a bridge, and others waded the river where the robbers had, but we saw nothing of them that day, although we were satisfied that they were in some of the thickets in that vicinity.

About eight o'clock that night we discovered them, after they had come out of a thicket, crossing an open space of prairie to another thicket, about seven hundred yards away. Captain McDonald, Billy McCauley, Jack Harvell, Bob McClure and Lee Queen entered the north side, and I the south side, and we all came upon the robbers about the same time, and demanded their surrender. When we found their sixshooters on the ground, a few minutes later, we discovered they were cocked, which showed that they came very near fighting us. They had their Winchesters hidden at Wichita Falls, but after they robbed the bank, and were leaving town, the citizens prevented the men from getting them.

We recovered the money they had taken from the bank—six hundred and seventy-seven dollars and ten cents—and then went to a house close by and got supper, after which we returned to Wichita Falls, arriving there about four o'clock in the morning. We guarded the jail the remainder of the night and all the next day, and, as everything seemed to be perfectly quiet, and as there were no signs of trouble, we left that evening on the north-bound train for our headquarters at Amarillo.

When we reached Childress we received a telegram stating that two thousand citizens were breaking into the jail. When we reached Clarendon we received another telegram stating that they had hung the robbers.

The citizens of Wichita Falls got twelve hundred dollars of the reward, and the other rangers and I received the rest—eight hundred dollars.

A few days later I went back to Wichita Falls, where I met Elmer Lewis' mother. She was standing at the head of the table, watching me while I ate my dinner, and when I had finished, she asked me to come into her room, as she wanted to talk with me. After we entered, and she had closed and thumb-bolted the door, she asked me to take a rocking chair.

"No, I do not care to sit in a rocker," I answered, "for I had a rib broken not long ago, and it pains me when I sit in a rocker."

"I have been wanting to see you ever since I came to Texas," she said, "I am Elmer Lewis' mother. Where were you at the time Elmer was hung?"

"I was at Childress."

"How far is that from here?"

"About one hundred and twenty miles," I replied, "but I was at Clarendon, sixty miles further up the road, when I received the news that the two men were hung."

"If you had been here, do you think you could have prevented the hanging?"

"I think not, as they were two thousand strong."

"Of course, if that was the case, you could not have prevented it," she replied.

"The jailer has my watch, that my son had," she continued, "and I wish you would get it for me."

"How old are you, Mrs. Lewis?"

"I am thirty-six," she answered.

"You are so young looking that the people here do not believe you are Elmer Lewis' mother."

"Well, you see I am Scotch-Irish, and you know we hold our age well."

She asked me again about the watch, and I told her that if it was her watch she should have it.

She then asked me to show her the way Lewis and Crawford went after they robbed the bank, and I pointed out the way to her, but never took my eyes off her; for when she bolted the door it made me somewhat suspicious, and when she asked me to have a rocking chair, it made me more so; for she knew that if I sat in a rocker I could not get to my pistol easily, and I concluded she had not asked me in her room for any good purpose, as she kept her hands under her apron all the time. She then asked me for my address, thinking, probably, I would lower my head while writing it, but I had an envelope in my pocket which had my address written on it; so I took the letter out and handed her the envelope, watching her all the time. We talked a while longer, and when I arose to leave, I walked backward to the door, keeping my eyes on her while I unlocked it, and then told her good-bye.

I believe it was her intention to kill me, as she tried every way to get me to take my eyes off her; but I was on the lookout.

The watch, which she spoke of, was advertised in a newspaper, and a man and his wife came from Oklahoma and identified it, telling the jailer it had three letters in it, and that they were very dim, but could be seen upon close inspection, which proved true. They said the watch had been stolen from them. It did not belong to Mrs. Lewis. I received two letters from her, after she went back to Missouri, in regard to the watch. I learned from the sheriff of her county that she was Elmer Lewis' mother, notwithstanding the fact that she looked so young.

XLI

A CALL TO HARTLEY

In 1897, while a detachment of us ranger boys were stationed in Hartley, looking after crime (as Hartley, at that time, was a very tough place, full of thieves and other bad characters, gambling and all kinds of lawlessness going on day and night), I was told that a man, in the back end of a saloon in a private room, was playing cards and putting up United States stamps in the place of money. I went into the room and looked on and saw him lose six dollars and seventy-five cents worth of stamps. I asked him if he was a postmaster. He stated that he was. I asked him where he was from. He said, "From Coldwater, Texas." I told him that I guess I would have to arrest him, as I was satisfied he was not a postmaster, and that he had stolen those stamps.

After I had arrested him, he then told me that he was a deputy postmaster, and then I was satisfied that he had robbed that postoffice of these stamps. I held him in Hartley for a few days, until I could find out from the postmaster of Coldwater if this man was his deputy. The postmaster answered that he was, and that he had robbed the office of these stamps, and for me to be sure and hold him, and he said this man also had a negro woman for his wife. I wired the United States Marshal at Wichita Falls that I was holding this man for robbing the postoffice at Coldwater. We had no jail or calaboose in Hartley; so I kept him under guard three days and nights. Then I took him to Amarillo, and placed him in jail for the nearest marshal to come and get. Before leaving Hartley I learned that his negro wife was on a visit in Amarillo; so after reaching Amarillo and placing him in jail, I thought it a good idea to hunt his negro wife. There were only six or eight negroes living in Amarillo. I located the house in which she was stopping, and found that three men and three negro women were stopping at this place. I knocked on the door, and someone inside told me to come in. I went in and asked, "Which one of you women is Mrs. Joe Jackson?"

A yellow negro woman answered and said, "I am Mrs. Joe Jackson."

Then I told her that I had come from Coldwater, and had met her husband, Mr. Joe Jackson. "When I left Coldwater," I continued, "your husband told me to hunt you up, saying that he was very sick at Coldwater."

She said she was very sorry, and that she was glad I had informed her, and that she would take the first train for Coldwater. I then told her that her husband had told me the county they had married in. She told me that it was in Burleson County, Texas. I told her that I liked her husband very much, and that I thought he was a nice gentleman. She stated that he was very good and kind to her. I told her that he had told me who married them in Burleson County, but I had forgotten. She said old Squire Blackburn had married them. She also stated he had two brothers, and also had two sisters, and that his father was dead; that his brothers, sisters, and mother disliked it so much for him to marry her, that they left at once for Coldwater, and had been there ever since they had married. After getting the information from her that they were legally married, I then arrested her and placed her in jail, where I had placed her husband about one hour and a half before. When I got the jailer up, about one or two o'clock in the night, he opened the door, and she spoke. Her husband recognized her voice from his cell and asked, "Is that you, Annie?" and she answered, "It is." Then she asked, "Is that you, Joe?" and he answered that it was. "This officer has got me arrested," she replied, "and told me he met you in Coldwater, and that you were very sick, and stated for me to hurry home, and he got me to make a statement about us being married, and after making my statement he arrested me." That gave the State a case, as it was a violation of the law for a white man and a negro woman to marry in Texas.

XLII

ON THE TRAIL OF TRAIN ROBBERS

While in Amarillo I was notified, in 1899, by the Adjutant General, that a train was robbed at Benbrook, fourteen miles from Fort Worth, on the T. & P. Railroad. J. V. Goode, superintendent of the Fort Worth & Denver, had a car sent for our horse and saddles. After loading the horses and saddles on, we crawled into the caboose, and the car was hitched onto the south-bound passenger train, and we arrived in Fort Worth on schedule time.

Sheriff Eulis, of Tarrant County, joined us at Fort Worth, and Superintendent Thorn, of the T. & P. Railroad, had our car hitched to an engine and we left immediately for Weatherford. Everything between Fort Worth and Weatherford was side-tracked, and, having an open track all the way, we made a quick run, arriving at our destination that evening. We unloaded our horses and saddles, and spent the night in Weatherford.

The following morning we were joined by the sheriff of Parker County, and all of us started out together to look for the robbers. At Springtown the sheriff of Tarrant County had to leave and go back to Fort Worth.

We searched the whole country around Weatherford, finally striking the trail of two men, who were well armed, each having two belts of cartridges, a Winchester, and sixshooter. One of the men was mounted on an iron grey stallion, while the other

Edgar T. Neal   Allen Maddox   Tom Johnson, Cook   Dud Barker   W. J. L. Sullivan

"Sullivan's Ranger Camp on the banks of San Saba River, near San Saba Town,"

was mounted on a black, bald face, stocking leg horse.

We followed the trail of these two men, and struck the Fort Worth & Denver road at the town of Sunset. While crossing the country, near Red River, I lost the trail, but I learned that a Joe Couch had loaned an iron grey horse to a stranger about two weeks before the robbery, and had never seen it since. I looked for Couch, but failed to find him. I decided that the robbers were playing fox on us and had turned back; so we dropped back, too, going to Decatur, and tried there to get all the information that we could concerning the fugitives.

While I was in Decatur, I had occasion to call up Irby Duncan, in Fort Worth, on a little business, and Col. R. D. Hunter, president of the T. & P. Coal Company, got the other end of the line for a few minutes, and asked me how I was getting along with the train robbers.

I told him that I had lost their trail, and it did not look like I was going to find it again.

He asked me if I had been notified that the Rock Island had been held up and robbed the night before.

I told him that I had not; so he notified S. B. Hoovey, superintendent of the Rock Island, that I was in Decatur with six rangers. I asked Col. Hunter to have Captain McDonald, who was in Fort Worth at that time, found and brought to the phone. McDonald gave me a little more information about the Rock Island hold-up, and I quit the trail of the Benbrook robbers at once, and went to work on this other case.

I went to Bridgeport, reaching there in a few minutes, and found transportation, which Superintendent Hoovey had sent me. A little later on Hoovey came up to Bridgeport from Fort Worth on the train that was to pull us to Red River. Hoovey and I discussed the situation at some length.

Before leaving Bridgeport, I found Joe Couch, the one who loaned one of the Benbrook robbers a grey horse. I found him playing cards, and I took him and his horse with me on the train to Red River.

Reaching Red River, I learned that the robbers had boarded the train on the Texas side, and while the train was crossing the river they relieved the passengers of all their money and jewelry. Arriving in the little town of Harrel, on the other side of the river, we discovered that the officers of that community had captured the robbers and placed them in the depot, where they were kept under guard. We put the prisoners and the officers, who had them in charge, on our train and took them to Duncan. The marshal of that town claimed the men, but they were given over to the Texas authorities, and we put them in jail in the town of Montague, in Texas. They were tried twice, and succeeded in beating their cases. I was on hand at the trial, and we encountered lots of toughs, who were in town to intimidate the court and get their friends clear.

I was satisfied that these men were the same men who had held up the train at Benbrook, and I told the others that. I received a letter from Sheriff Pat Ware, of Cooke County, that there was an iron grey stallion in the livery stable at Gainesville; so I went at once to that town and had the sheriff point the horse out to me. I also asked the sheriff if he knew the man's whereabouts, and he said he thought he was across the river in the Indian Territory. I learned before I left headquarters camp a second time, that this grey stallion belonged to a man at Henrietta.

Pat Ware and I went across the river to look for this man, who had stolen the grey stallion, and about seven miles on the other side we learned that there was a suspicious looking stranger picking cotton at a certain farm. We went at once to this place, and, going into the field, we saw a cluster of men, all picking cotton.

I had never seen the man before, but ever since I had been on his trail the first time, I had had him described to me so often, that I knew him before Pat and I had gotten close to him. Pat also knew the man from the description I had given of him.

He surrendered to us, without any trouble on our part, and we asked him, in the presence of several witnesses all around him, if he was willing to go across the line without any requisition.

He said that he was; so we handcuffed him, and, hiring a horse, we left with him at once for Gainesville.

When he neared the river, he remarked that he believed that he would not cross the line without a requisition. We told him that we would show him whether he would cross over or not, as he had said before fifteen or twenty witnesses that he would go into Texas with us without requisition. He then went on to Gainesville with us without any further trouble. We gave him a bed in the Gainesville jail that night, and took him the next morning to Henrietta, where we notified the owner of the grey horse that he could get his property. Our prisoner was wanted for selling mortgaged mules, as well as for stealing this horse.

The Benbrook train robbers, whom we came so near capturing several times, were finally caught in Fort Worth by local officers.

XLIII

THE SAN SABA MOB

In 1896 I was ordered by Governor Culberson to go to San Saba and put down the mob that had existed there for sixteen years. Governor Culberson sent me because he knew I was well posted with this mob, for I had been sent there in 1890, as stated in a preceding chapter, to preserve order while court was going on. I had also been a witness in the Campbell case ever since then, and was familiar with all the leading people on both sides of the wrangle.

By this time the situation had reached a very perplexing stage in San Saba. The men of both factions were very bitter and aggressive. Good and bad citizens, both, were on either side. In their continued strife both factions had lost sight of the lofty ideals (which had probably at first actuated them), and now allowed their animal passions to overcome them. The mob people had originally organized to put down lawlessness, while the "anti-mobists" had organized to oppose mobism, because they thought the law should be allowed to take its own course; but those first principles had long been forgotten. Lawless people had joined both factions, and had introduced their evil influences among members of each side.

When the mob was first organized it started out by preventing crime, especially stealing, but now lawlessness was being encouraged by both sides, and could not be suppressed by local authorities.

The bitterness between the two factions had become so great that a number of murders occurred, and were traced to one or the other side. The State finally had to step in and put down the strife by suppressing the mob, as that was the side which was arrayed against the law. Cattle thieves, murderers and other criminals were also given prompt attention, irrespective of the faction to which they belonged.

When we went to San Saba, I took Dud Barker from Company B, and Captain J. H. Rogers sent me two men from his company—Edgar T. Neal and Allen Maddox. Barker and I were joined by the two other rangers, Neal and Maddox, when we reached Goldthwaite. Sheriff Hudson, of San Saba also met us at Goldthwaite with a wagon and team. The three rangers under me went to San Saba in the wagon, and Sheriff Hudson took me over in his buggy.

The county furnished me with a wagon, harness, and a span of mules, and the State furnished me a cook. We spent three days in the town of San Saba, and then left for Hannah's Crossing, on the Colorado River.

That was a beautiful place to camp, and that part of the river was one of the finest fishing spots in the world. We remained there four months, and enjoyed our stay, except for the danger we were in when we first arrived there.

The people of both factions, especially the mob element, were antagonistic to us when we first went to San Saba, and our lives were in danger. When we four boys pitched our tent at Hannah's Crossing, we shook hands with each other and made a solemn pledge that we would stay there and do our duty if we all had to die together. We vowed that we would arrest anybody of either faction, whom we caught disobeying the law, and that we would die working the lever of our guns before we would give up our prisoners, no matter how many men we had to fight.

When we pitched our camp, we expected that we would never have to move it again; for it seemed to me that we were doomed to die at the hands of some of the people of the bad element, who were indignant at our coming to San Saba. We went about our work quietly, however, and made friends with everybody we could, and showed them that we were not after anybody but those who maliciously violated the law. The better class of people soon began to treat us kindly, and we were often invited to take dinner with them. We always accepted their invitations, and would eat one day with a member of the mob, and the next day we would probably dine with some one of the anti-mob faction. We showed no partiality to either side, and in that way we gained the respect of the law-abiding citizens of both factions, and our stay in San Saba was, for the most part, quite pleasant. With the tough characters, however, we had some rough times, and I met with quite a number of thrilling experiences, some of which I shall relate in following chapters.

Hannah's Crossing was twenty miles from San Saba, on the San Saba & Brownwood Railroad. When we went out to it, we were accompanied by Sheriff Hudson, who stayed at our camp a day or two before he went back to town. We located in Jim Linsey's pasture, which was near the river.

A week before we pitched camp, three men concealed themselves in this pasture one day and assassinated Bill James, a well-known citizen, while the latter was going after water in his wagon. We tried to capture the assassins, but they had a week's start on us; so we gave up, as we had lots of other work to do, and left it to the county officials to ferret out the perpetrators of the James murder.

During the trouble between the two factions in San Saba, a Mr. Turner, an anti-mobist, was killed, and, it was alleged, that he was murdered by Matt Ford and Tobe Bridge, two members of the mob. The trial, which took place at Austin, was sensational, and created state-wide interest. Ford and Bridge were defended by Governor Hogg, Judge James Robertson, and Judge Pendexter, of Austin, and Attorneys John and Ab Walters, brothers, of San Saba. They were as good lawyers as the State afforded. Judge Albert Burleson and W. C. Linden were the prosecuting attorneys. There were 369 witnesses. Judge Morris was the district judge. The two men were at last acquitted, and went back home to live, and they led a different life and made good citizens.

The two factions in San Saba finally made peace with each other and buried the hatchet. The last time I was with them they were going to church and visiting each other, and all signs of former strife and bad feeling had faded away.

XLIV

A BAD DOG.

I was summoned from San Saba, where I was at work putting down a mob, to Wellington, Collingsworth County, to appear against some cattle thieves. While in Wellington I was presented with a large dog, which weighed a hundred and ten or fifteen pounds. He was a hound, and looked to be very ferocious.

I thought it would be a good idea to take him to San Saba, pass him off as a fine bloodhound, and get the people afraid of him, as that would help me to put down some of the lawlessness that reigned there.

When I went to Fort Worth, I bought a fine collar and two chains for him. I named my dog "Bill." I expressed him to Lometa, where he and I were to take the stage to San Saba.

I put both chains on Bill, to make people think he was very hard to hold. When we arrived at Lometa, I chained the dog to the stage. He reared and surged against the chains furiously, and acted like he would tear the earth up if he could get loose, but it was all nothing but pretensions, for the dog really was no account for anything. When he reared around, growled, showed his teeth, and tried to break the chains, he looked as dangerous as a lion; and I was glad of it, for I wanted him to fool the people, and make them think I had a dog that would tear them up if he was sent after them when they committed crime. He reminded me of a man who seems anxious to get into a fight, although deathly afraid of the other fellow.

The stage driver was afraid of Bill and would not go near him.

That night at ten o'clock an old nestor from the the woods walked up to the stage to get a jug of syrup that he had sent for that morning. When Bill got scent of the old man and his two dogs, he at once got on the warpath and charged around like a lion. The stage driver said to the man:

"Please do not come any nearer. Sullivan has his bloodhound on the stage, and he is about to turn everything over now. If he should break loose he might kill you and your dogs too. I will set your jug of syrup down, and when I drive away you can get it."

This break of Bill's gave him a big reputation as a ferocious bloodhound to start off with. The stage driver asked me to give him Bill's record, and he also wanted to know where I got such a fine dog.

I did not inform the stage driver that Bill was a worthless dog; that he had been raised on the streets of Wellington, but I told him he had been given to me by a friend of mine who lived in New York. I told him that Bill had done wonderful work for the officials at Sing Sing, in running down the most noted criminals in the United States.

The people in the stage gasped at that, and I told them that I would use Bill on the criminals in San Saba.

I felt it my duty to tell the people these tales about this dog, for the odds were against me in San Saba, and my life would not be in so much danger if the people were afraid of Bill. Besides that, some people might refrain from committing crime, for fear this dog would catch them, and either hurt them or bring them to justice.

I reached San Saba about twelve o'clock that night, and put up at the hotel. By the next morning the news had spread all over the country about me bringing Bill with me, and people flocked in from every direction to see Bill. They asked me all kinds of questions about him, and, time and again, I told them his whole wonderful history.

They asked me to let him chase somebody, but I told them that he was in San Saba for straight business, and not for foolishness. "At the proper time," I said, "he will show his blood; but the main reason why I don't let him chase someone for fun, is that he might kill somebody, and I do not want to be responsible for anything like that."

They thought that was a good reason, and they were more afraid of him than ever.

I was detained so long by the people who wanted to see Bill that I didn't reach my camp until that afternoon. I kept my dog with me at Hannah's Crossing, and the people all up and down the river came to my camp to see him. I kept his fine collar on him, and he looked very vicious as he reared against the two chains and snapped and snarled at the visitors and showed his big, sharp teeth.

I cautioned the people not to get too close to him, telling them that he was not a play-dog. I also told them not to look too hard at him, for fear he would break the chains and tear somebody up before I could get him under control. The people minded me very well, and I never did have any trouble between them and the dog.

Not a single murder occurred while I had Bill, and I had no occasion to use him, for which I was very thankful, as Bill would have proved an absolute failure had I ever unchained him and set him off after a criminal.

XLV

A GOOD TIME LOST

One Sunday morning while we were camping at Hannah's Crossing, all four of us rangers—Edgar Neal, Allen Maddox, Dud Barker and I—were invited across the river to participate in a "Hardshell Baptist foot-washing."

We accepted the invitation, and enjoyed the meeting very much. The members of the congregation asked us to stay with them for dinner, as they were to have a spread on the grounds, and they desired very much to have us eat with them. They were to introduce us boys to the young people, and we were intending to have a very sociable afternoon. We had told the people that we would eat with them, and had made arrangements to stay all day; but just as the doxology was being sung, our cook, whom we called Tom, came to the church in "fool's haste," lit off his horse at the church door, and asked a man who was sitting on a back seat to get us rangers for him.

We went out as soon as the man said that Tom wanted us. Tom informed us that there were two men at camp who desired very much to see us, and for us to go as quickly as possible.

We made a break for our horses, jumped into our saddles, and made a three-mile run in a few minutes, believing all the time that when we reached camp we would hear that someone in the neighborhood had been killed.

When we arrived at our destination we found

the two men waiting for us. One of them said he wanted to speak to me. He took me off where the others couldn't hear him, and, in whispers, told me that on the day before, while he was in the cotton patch, someone had entered his smokehouse and stolen twelve pounds of bacon. I told him at once that if it wasn't Sunday I would hang him for causing us rangers to run our horses nearly to death, besides missing our dinner and a good time with the young people, just because he had twelve pounds of bacon stolen from him. We offered to go and see about the theft, however, and the next morning we got our horses and started over to his place, which was about nine miles from camp.

While riding along the road we got thirsty, so we stopped in at a house and got a drink of water. When we entered the yard we saw two ladies in the hallway of the house sewing on a quilt. When we asked their permission to get a drink of water, one of the ladies politely told us to come in and help ourselves, which we did.

After we had finished drinking, she seated us, and said she thought she knew where we were going.

"Maybe you do," I said, in a manner that invited her to speak on and tell us what was in her mind.

"I think you are going to see about some bacon that was stolen last Saturday afternoon," she replied.

"Yes, we have started over that way," I said.

"I have no idea," she continued, "that anyone stole that bacon. The smokehouse door was left open, and I think the dog went in and dragged a few pounds of meat out. The man married a mere child, and I suppose she left the door open herself, when she went down to the field to see her husband."

When the old lady got through talking, I spoke up and asked, "Why didn't the crazy man marry a woman that was old enough and had sense enough to keep house for him."

"His wife is my daughter," she replied, and then the rangers had the laugh on me.

Conversation between the old lady and me then ceased for a few minutes, and I thought of the good time I would have had Sunday, and the trouble I would have been saved, if those two men had not ridden nine miles to our camp, and made the cook ride three more miles and summon all four of us rangers, and cause us to ride nine miles and back for nothing the next day; all because a dog had stolen ten or twelve pounds of bacon.

As we expected, we found no bacon thief, and went back to camp feeling rather done up, and wishing to forget the incident as long as we lived.

XLVI

FORDING THE RIVER

Soon after dark one evening, while we were camping at Hannah's Crossing, I received a message from the postmaster at Indian Creek, in Brown County, saying that the postoffice at that place had been robbed. I was urged to go to the scene of the robbery at once; so we packed one of the mules and immediately started for Indian Creek.

It was very dark, and rain was pouring down in torrents, but we went on anyway, and tried to find a place where we could ford the river, as we wanted to cross it before daylight.

We went up the river about twelve miles, but still could find no place where we thought it was safe to cross. We feared that it was raining so hard further up the river that we couldn't cross any better up there than where we were, so we decided to stay at Bill Martin's house, which was nearby, until daylight.

We went up to Mr. Martin's house and called him to the door.

He asked me who we were.

I told him that I was Sullivan, and that I had the Texas rangers with me.

It was raining so hard that it was only with difficulty that we could hear each other talk. Martin invited us to spend the night in the house with him, but we told him we couldn't stop unless it was impossible for us to ford the river.

W. J. L. SULLIVAN

Marshal of the Day at the Cowboys' Reunion at Seymour—20,000 Whites and 503 Comanches present. Held four days and nights, perfect order maintained.

We then asked him if he thought we could make it safely to the other side.

In reply, he said that if it has rained above as it has here, the river is bound to be "swimming," and that he would advise us not to cross the river tonight. He again invited us to spend the night in the house with him, but we were so wet that we decided it wouldn't do for us to go in and sleep in his beds and get them damp; so I asked Mr. Martin to let us sleep in his gin-house, since we could not cross the river, and did not want to go in his house in our condition.

He assured us that that would be perfectly agreeable to him; so we went into the gin, and each one of us dug a hole in the cotton and slept in it. The next morning, when we got up, we found that the heat of the cotton had nearly dried us.

Mr. Martin and his wife fixed a good breakfast for us, and as long as I live I shall never forget that big dish of fried chicken and that pot of delicious coffee that they had prepared for us.

After breakfast we went to the river to see if it was very high, and found that it was just about "swimming." It looked silly for wise men to plunge into that river; but we four boys split it wide open, leading our pack mule, and crossed safely over to the other side.

We reached Indian Creek that day, and captured the men who had robbed the postoffice. I sent them to Brownwood by Barker and Maddox, and they stood trial for the robbery and beat the case. Edgar Neal and I remained in that community several days looking up testimony for the State.

XLVII

GIRLS TRY TO KISS NEAL

While looking up testimony in the country around Indian Creek, a few days after the post-office robbery, Edgar Neal and I came to a house where a Mrs. Hogan, a widow, and her four daughters lived. It was about an hour and a half before sun-down when we arrived at Mrs. Hogan's house. We had learned before reaching this place that the two men whom we had arrested had stopped there the night they committed the postoffice robbery. Mrs. Hogan said that they left her house that night at eleven o'clock. She also informed us that the two men lived directly east of her, and when they left the house the night of the robbery they climbed over the fence and went due west, the direction of the postoffice. The evidence that we had accumulated that day and the things Mrs. Hogan told us that evening, led us to believe that we had arrested the right parties.

When we first went into her house and seated ourselves, Mrs. Hogan asked us if we were strangers in that part of the country. I replied that we were, and I told her my name. She gave me her name, and treated me in a cordial manner. I saw at once that they were well-to-do, cultured people, and, after introducing myself, I presented Mr. Neal to Mrs. Hogan.

"Mrs. Hogan," I said, "allow me to introduce you to Mr. Neal."

"Is it Bedgar Neal?" she asked.

"It is," Edgar answered.

"My dear nephew," she joyfully exclaimed, "why didn't you let me know you when you first came in? I thought I recognized those eyes when you first stepped in at the door."

She made a dive at Edgar, and grabbed him by the hand. She looked like she was trying to kiss him, but he leaned his head out of her reach. Then she asked him how "Dona and the baby were." He replied that they were both well.

"You have fleshened up mightily," she said.

He nodded.

I was just about to tell the old lady that she was mistaken in this man, when she called out to her four daughters, who were in the next room, and said, "Come in, girls, Cousin Bedgar is here."

All four of them came hopping and skipping in at once, and they were as pretty as any girls I ever saw. I was wishing that they would make some mistake about me; but they didn't; Edgar got the benefit of it all.

The lady introduced the girls to him, for fear he had forgotten some of their names. Then they began to hanging on him, and trying to kiss him. He played the same game on them, however, that he played on the old lady; he ducked his head and leaned it over to one side.

After they got through hugging each other, Edgar and the four girls sat down together in the middle of the room.

One of the girls asked Edgar how Dona and the baby were.

He replied that they were both well.

"You have fleshened up so we like to have not

known you," another girl observed, when she had a chance to speak.

Now, while all this was going on, my heart was beating like a mule kicking down hill. I was frightened. I knew if they discovered their mistake and found out this was not "Cousin Bedgar," that they would make it hot for us, for the old lady had a game appearance, and, also, the four girls; so I kept asking questions about the robbers, for fear they would keep talking to Edgar and get him tangled up and learn that he was fooling them. Whenever they asked Edgar a difficult question, I broke into the conversation and asked some important question about the robbers, thus saving Edgar from answering their queries.

Finally it got to where I could stand it no longer, and I said, "Ladies, we will have to be traveling, as we are on urgent business."

The old lady and all four girls spoke up and said at once, "Cousin Bedgar, you are not going to leave us now, are you?" Holding to his arms and coat, they continued, "Cousin Bedgar, you have not been here in so long, you cannot leave here tonight."

I spoke up and said, "We are forced to go, ladies. We will return tomorrow evening and spend the night," and Edgar said, "Yes we will. I see you have a piano, and we will sing and play." The old lady said, "My dear boy, you should not leave your aunt tonight."

We were both satisfied that we had spent about all the time we could spare at that place; so, after telling the family good-bye, we quickly made for our horses. We laughed a great deal about the joke on Mrs. Hogan, and often wondered how we came out of it alive. We learned afterward that they enjoyed the joke very much, and when the girls first realized that their mother had caused them to be fooled, they took it good-naturedly, and in a spirit of fun, they pounded her considerably on the back.

Edgar Neal enjoyed jokes immensely, and was a good-hearted man. He quit the ranger company at San Saba and became the sheriff of that county, making the people a splendid officer during the eight years that he served them.

XLVIII

THE CAPTURE OF WAX LEE

While I was stationed at San Saba, Tom Grey, a hardware man of that town, received a letter addressed to a man with his name. Upon opening it, he saw that it was written by someone in Paris, and was meant for another "Tom Grey."

In this letter the Paris man warned his friend in San Saba that the officers were still looking for him, and that he had "gone to a mighty good place to get caught." The letter also revealed the fact that the man's real name was Wax Lee, and that "Tom Grey" was his alias.

When Mr. Grey, the merchant, told me about the letter, I knew at once that the other "Tom Grey" was badly wanted somewhere; so I went to the postoffice and waited for someone to call for the letter.

Late that evening Mr. Jim Brooks, brother to Judge Brooks of Austin, came to the postoffice and called for the letter which was addressed to Tom Grey. I asked Mr. Brooks if he knew anyone by the name of Tom Grey. He replied that he had a man by that name working for him, and that Grey had a companion with him.

Brooks lived about twelve miles out of town; so I got a buggy and went out to his place. Brooks went in the buggy with me, and I sent the three ranger boys out there on horseback. I hadn't recovered from the injuries, which I received while chasing Del Dean, and was not able to ride horseback.

When we reached the farm Brooks led us to an old house, where the two men were camping. We could not get the buggy right up to the house, however, on account of a slough, which emptied into the Colorado River, and which lay between us and the house. This slough was so muddy and boggy that I could not get the buggy across, as I have stated before; so I sent the three other rangers over on their horses, and told them to capture the men and be very careful in making the arrests.

After the boys had gone I discovered a tent about forty yards in front of me, and thinking that the man I wanted might possibly be in it, I got out of the buggy, and, leaving Brooks to hold the horses, I walked toward the tent to see what I could find. Brooks had told me that Lee was dark complected, and when I had nearly reached the tent, a man of that description came to the door. I decided to arrest him, but, when I started toward him, Jim Brooks called out and told me that the boys had arrested the men; so I whirled around and went back to the buggy. When the rangers got back to the buggy I saw that Brooks was mistaken, for the boys had captured only one man, and he was the companion of the one I was after. Brooks saw and heard the rangers when they made the arrest, but took it for granted that they had captured two men instead of one, and, being thus mistaken, he informed me wrong.

When I turned and walked away from the tent, Wax Lee, the man whom I started to arrest, broke and ran toward the river, crossed the slough, and hid in the brush, which was thick all along there. I saw the man running, and when the rangers turned their prisoner, a young fellow, over to me, I told them to go after the other man immediately.

I mounted Brooks and sent him along with them, as I knew they would have a hard time finding the man, if he hid in the brush, and they would need all the help they could get.

As I was afraid he would do, the man hid in the brush, and the boys couldn't find him anywhere. After searching the brush a little while they gave it up, and got together to plan what was the best move to make next. During the conference, Dud Barker discovered that while he was loping his horse a few minutes before that, his sixshooter had worked around too far behind him, and while talking to the other man he reached around and pulled his gun in front of his belt to readjust it. None of the men knew that Wax Lee lay hidden within a few feet of them while they were wondering where he had gone to, and Lee could not understand what the men were saying; so when he saw them stop, he thought he had been discovered, but decided to lie still, thinking that he might be mistaken. When he saw Dud Barker pull his pistol in front on his belt, however, he thought that he had surely been discovered, and imagined that Barker was going to shoot him, so he called out and asked the rangers not to kill him. He then surrendered to the boys, who were very much surprised, since they had not seen him before he crawled out of the brush.

The rangers fired their sixshooters, to let me know that they had captured their man. When

I heard the shots, however, I was afraid that they were having a battle with Lee, but pretty soon they brought him up, and we took the two prisoners to town.

When the boys brought him up to the buggy, Lee told me that he was satisfied just as soon as he saw I was after him, that I had his right name. He then told me that his name was Wax Lee, and that that was his son whom we captured with him.

When we reached San Saba with the prisoners we learned that Wax Lee and his son were wanted in Paris, Texas, and also in the Indian Territory. We wired the sheriff at Paris, telling him that we had his prisoners. The two men were charged with four murders and twenty thefts of horses and cattle. The sheriff at Paris gave us a hundred dollars for the capture. A big reward was out for the men in the Indian Territory, and we tried to get it, but some slick scoundrel beat us out of it.

XLIX

THE COWBOYS' REUNION

Judge Glascow, of Seymour, notified me, while I was in Austin in 1897, that I was elected Marshal of the Day over the Cowboys' Reunion, which was to be held in his town on the 3rd, 4th, 5th and 6th days of August. Later on Judge Glascow came to Austin, and I met him at the Avenue Hotel. I was then attending court, aiding in the trial of the famous Matt Ford and Tobe Bridge murder case, which was removed from San Saba to Austin.

Judge Glascow asked me if I had received his letter, in which he had notified me that I was to be the Marshal of the Day at the Cowboys' Reunion in August.

I told him that I had received the letter, and he asked me if I wasn't going to serve them.

I told them that I would be proud to do so, but that I would have to see McDonald, my captain.

"Where is Bill?" he asked.

"There he is, just a few steps from you," I answered.

Glascow walked up to McDonald and told him that a committee had elected me to act as Marshal of the Day over the Cowboys' Reunion at Seymour, and asked him if I could serve them.

McDonald replied that I could not go, as I would have too much work to do then putting down the mob which was raging in San Saba County.

"You are over Sullivan as captain," Glascow replied, "but there are two men at the Capitol over you, and I shall go to see them."

Glascow then walked up to the Capitol and was gone about a half hour. When he returned to the hotel, he tapped me on the shoulder and said, "Charley Culberson, the Governor of our State, and W. H. Mabry, the Adjutant General, both say that you shall act as marshal at the Cowboys' Reunion."

I left for Seymour in time to arrive there by the night of the 2nd of August, and the following morning I was sworn in as Marshal of the Day.

Twenty thousand white people and five hundred Comanches were in Seymour for the reunion. Chief Quanah Parker had charge of the Comanches. I served them four days and nights as an officer and never jailed a single person. The whole town was turned loose to the cowboys and other visitors. There never was better behavior known in such a large crowd before.

Thirty saloons were open day and night, and the cowboys drank some and had lots of fun, but they were as quiet as necessary and respected the law. On the night of the 5th the Indians gave a great war dance on the reunion grounds that was quite an interesting sight to witness. I had to arrest a man for cutting the rope that was stretched around the arena in which the Indians danced, but his wife and mother and two young ladies, who were with him, all plead so earnestly in his behalf that I didn't lock him up, but let him go free.

Judge Glascow, ex-sheriff Sam Suttlemeyer of Baylor County, Quanah Parker and his favorite wife, and I had our photographs taken together. Quanah stole this squaw from another Comanche, and his men got mad and deserted him and he went to New Mexico, where they stayed several months. The Comanche, whose wife was stolen from him, finally wrote to the Chief and told him if he would give him eleven hundred dollars he could keep her and could come back and take charge of his tribe. Quanah at once paid the money, and again became the Chief of the Comanches. I found Quanah and his men to be easily controlled, and they gave me no trouble whatever.

One night after the reunion had closed for the day, and while the people were on their way from the fair grounds to the city, about two thousand cowboys bunched up together and commenced firing their sixshooters off in the air. The guns gleamed in the moonlight, and it looked like the world was full of lightning bugs. Quanah and several of his braves rushed up to me on their horses and asked me what the shooting meant. I told them that it was a lot of jolly cowboys having a little fun, but meaning no harm. Quanah and his Comanches were on the reunion grounds, and I told Quanah to call his men together and have them form themselves in a circle. They did as I had requested, and all got as close together as possible, and I held them that way until the cowboys had passed and ceased their shooting. There was no danger of the cowboys making any break at the Indians, but I thought I had better take that precaution.

I witnessed during that reunion some of the finest roping and "broncho busting" that I ever saw in my life. I have often wished since then that I could witness another reunion like this, and be the marshal of the day, and have things move off as they did at Seymour.

L

HIDDEN WITNESSES

When I left the ranger service I accepted a deputyship under Sheriff Pearle of Williamson County. One day while court was in session at Georgetown, Judge D. S. Chesser told me that he had received a 'phone message form Corn Hill, saying that four suspicious characters were camping about ten miles from that place, and that some officers should go out and investigate the party. The man who 'phoned Judge Chesser had been out bee hunting, and when he walked near the camp, one of the four men motioned him not to come near them by waving a towel at him. The hunter became suspicious and 'phoned Judge Chesser. As all the officers were busy, Judge Chesser asked me to go out with him to round up the men and find out what they were doing in that pasture.

I told him that I would go with him, and we left a little after dark, reaching Corn Hill about eleven o'clock that night. A Mr. Johnson, the man who had sent for Judge Chesser, met us there, and, mounting his horse, went the rest of the way with us.

About three miles from Corn Hill, Johnson said that he knew a man down in the corn field who was very good and brave, and that it would be a good idea to take him along, as the place where the men were camped was surrounded by brush, and that they could easily escape if we didn't take another man along to help us. Though it looked rather funny to me, I consented to his getting this man from the corn field, but our new assistant seemed very willing to join us, so I had no regrets about it. He carried a muzzle-loading shotgun, the lock, stock and barrel of which were all three whitewashed.

Traveling a mile further on, we came to another house, and Johnson expressed the wish that we get the man who lived there to join us, so we pressed him in, too.

About three miles further on we stopped and got breakfast. We had lots of fried chicken to eat, and we did full justice to the occasion, as we had ridden all night and were dreadfully hungry.

Referring to the gentleman who was entertaining us, Judge Chesser, while at the breakfast table, spoke up and said: "We had better get this man to go along with us;" so I was now convinced that the Judge was in favor of plenty of company. The other two men promptly said that they thought it a good idea to get him to go along and help us, and I commenced wondering if all the men's feet were not getting cold.

We pressed our kind friend into service and left immediately after breakfast, in order to arrive at the camp of the suspicious characters by daylight, so we could find them asleep. We were riding fast, and the morning star was rising and shining brighter all the time.

Nearing our destination, we came to another house, where we found a man and his dogs in the cotton field, driving out a bunch of cattle that had broken into his field during the night.

The man, his dogs, and his cows with their bells

on, were kicking up such a terrible racket that Judge Chesser decided that we had better press this man into service also, but we had a hard time getting him to the fence. When he finally reached us, however, we told him that we wanted him to help us arrest a bunch of outlaws who were camped nearly a mile from his place. He took a chill at once and said he was sick. He told us, though, that he had a hired man sleeping out in the yard on a cot, and that he thought he would go with us. We woke the man up and told him what we wanted, and he said he would go with us alright, and reaching under his pillow he pulled out a .22-calibre Smith & Wesson revolver. I asked him if that was the only gun he had, and he replied that it was. I handed him my .45 Colt's revolver, and loaned my other one to the man with the whitewashed gun, leaving me with my Bill Cook Winchester, which was a plenty for me. I felt perfectly safe with my trusty Winchester, for I knew it had never gone back on me.

Arriving within two hundred yards of the four men's camp, we dismounted and tied our horses. We walked up a little trail, which carried us about a hundred and fifty yards nearer the camp. Then we stopped and commenced a discussion as to what we should do next. The morning star shone still brighter and brighter. We decided to lie still until daybreak. We heard a rooster crow in the camp, and I remarked that they must be movers.

Just as day was peeping upon us, I told them to keep still, and I would make a sneak of about thirty steps toward their camp. I gave them instructions to come to me, one at a time, as soon as

Judge Glasgow Too Nicey Quanah Parker W. J. L. Sullivan Ex-Sheriff Sam Suttlemeyer

"At the Cowboys' Reunion at Seymour, Texas."

they saw me stop, and they did exactly as I had told them. I made another sneak, and they came to me again, as they had done before. That put us within ten or twelve steps of the camp. The chickens saw us, and not knowing what to make of us, they did some tall talking with each other, and I thought they would wake the men up before they got through. One man did rise up, and, getting on his knees, he held his Winchester in his right hand and looked toward the west, but we had come from the east, and he failed to see us. I was in front of my men and could see this man when he got up, but they couldn't, as they were scattered out behind live oak bushes, and I never spoke to them about the man handling his Winchester.

"It is about daylight, and we had better be getting up," said the man on the ground to the other men, but none of the sleepers responded to his call. In a few moments the man who had spoken these words, himself, lay down on his stomach, and pretty soon had gone off into "the sweet by and by."

I motioned my men to follow me, and in another minute we had spread all over the camp. Two of the men were sleeping on the ground, and two in the wagon, but we captured all four of them with ease.

We learned from them that they were witnesses in the Owens rape case, which was then being tried in Georgetown. When they told me that they were witnesses in that case, and that Col. Makemson had them hidden out on the quiet, I asked Judge Chesser if they had any such names as these men gave as witnesses, and he replied that they did. I then turned them loose, and, knowing that they were caught up with, they went to town that day and reported at the courthouse. Col. Makemson told me to let his witnesses alone after that.

LI

THE HANGING OF MORRISON

On the 25th of October, 1899, I was invited by Sheriff Williams of Wilbarger County to go to Vernon and help him hang a preacher, who was sentenced to be executed on the 27th of that month for the alleged murder of his wife, whom he had poisoned with strychnine. I accepted the invitation, and left at once for Vernon, arriving there on the morning of the 26th. The sheriff immediately put me on the death watch, and I remained on guard until eleven o'clock that night.

The prisoner, Rev. G. E. Morrison, who was sentenced to be hung on the next day, was supposed to have murdered his wife at their home in Panhandle City, and had been brought to Vernon for trial on a change of venue. Although given the death penalty, he denied his guilt to the last; but the evidence was conclusive, and proved beyond doubt that he had fallen in love with another woman, and had poisoned his wife to get rid of her.

Though most people believed him to be guilty, there was a movement on foot to have Morrison's sentence commuted to a life term in the penitentiary. A few days before his execution, however, he and two of his fellow-prisoners attempted to escape by attacking Mr. Shies, the jailer, and trying to overpower him. While one of the prisoners had Shies "clinched," Morrison yelled to him to "kill the jailer." This news reached Governor

Sayers while Morrison's sister and two attorneys were kneeling at his feet, pleading with him to commute the prisoner's sentence to life imprisonment in the penitentiary. There was a possibility of Governor Sayers' yielding to their prayer, but he determined upon the other course after he received the message from the sheriff and learned how ugly Morrison had acted. On the evening of the 26th the sheriff at Vernon received a telegram from the Governor saying that he must hang Morrison on the following day.

Morrison listened to the sheriff, as the latter read to him the Governor's message, and replied that all had been done that was possible and that he guessed he would have to take it.

The next morning his sister went to the jail and wept over him. Later on another lady and a preacher joined her, and the three knelt together in prayer. Morrison also prayed until time for the execution. At twelve o'clock he stood on the scaffold and made his farewell speech. A few minutes later his body dropped through the trapdoor and his neck was broken.

Morrison apparently took a fancy to me, and left me a pair of suspenders and a matchbox for keepsakes. He also wrote me a letter the night before his death, which I had requested him to do, as I wanted it for a souvenir. Following is the letter as he wrote it:

"VERNON, TEXAS, OCT. 26, 1899.

"MR. SULLIVAN.

"DEAR SIR: You have asked me to write something that you can keep to remember the occasion of our meeting. I don't know what to say to you, but I hope the following may be entirely satisfactory.

"First, I believe in a future life, and I believe that men are punished for the sins of this life, and are rewarded for the good things.

"Second, I believe in a general judgment, and all must stand in that day before the bar of God and be judged. I believe I have the witness of God's spirit bearing witness with my own spirit, and believe that, though God allows man's law to take my life yet he saves me, and of the future I have no fears whatever.

"Now, good-bye, and may you ever be a champion of the right and an enemy of the wrong.

"Your well-wisher,

"G. E. MORRISON."

LII

A PRAYER

During the first part of the summer of 1901 I was riding the range of the LX and Turkey Track ranch, on the Canadian River, guarding that place against a band of cow thieves and horse thieves and outlaws who were terrorizing the citizens in that part of the State. On the 8th of July, things having quieted down considerably on the range, I went over to a small ranch which I owned further up the river, to take a little rest.

During the afternoon of that day, while lying on the bed idly and quietly thinking over my past life, it suddenly came to my mind that in two more days I would be fifty years old, as the 10th of July would be the fiftieth anniversary of my birth.

With that thought I fell into deeper meditation. I asked myself if I had accomplished anything good in life, or if I had ever bettered myself or had done anything to help mankind in general in my humble way. I smiled when I reflected that I had always been an honest, law-abiding citizen, so far as I knew how, and had ever tried to be a faithful officer; but another thought came to my mind, and I smiled no more. It is true, I had always been careful to do my duty to my State and to society, but had I not been very negligent of my duty to God?

Once, in 1872, while attending a religious meeting in the little town of Douglasville, Texas, I was profoundly impressed with the doctrines of Christianity, as they were earnestly expounded by the able minister of that place. I did not feel, however, that I had been converted, and was leaving the church at the close of the services with no idea of becoming religious, when some of the preachers and a young lady, who was then Miss Cora Howe, stopped me and asked me to go up and give my life to God. I told them that I had not been converted; that I had not received God's grace. They talked to me a long time about my soul, and slapped me on the back so hard that I thought they were trying to beat religion into me. They finally left me and went their way, and I went mine.

I still thought that I had not been converted, but a night or two after that, while riding back home after the close of one of the meetings which I had attended, and while deeply meditating on religious subjects, a happy feeling came over me that I cannot describe. Some young people were riding just in front of me, whose gayety and laughter did not harmonize with the mood that had suddenly taken possession of my mind; so I held my horse back until the distance was so increased between them and me that I was left alone with God.

Not in a church building, with men and women all around watching me, but there in that lonely spot, surrounded by Nature, and with God my only witness, I beheld, even through the darkness of the night, a great light, and I reached out in an effort to grasp that brilliant, dazzling thing. I don't suppose I could have reached it myself, but because I tried so hard to get the light it came to me, flooding my mind with spiritual understanding, and I gave my heart to my Maker. The rest of the story I do not like to confess. I lived as a good Christian would for three years; and, then, as lots of men do, I began to be careless, and gradually grew more and more negligent of my duty to God, and for twenty-five years I left Him almost entirely out of my life and consideration. In other respects I had performed my duty and built up a good character, but I had not given God His due; and, as I lay on the bed on this July afternoon in 1901, these thoughts troubled my mind and pricked my conscience. I resolved that in two more days, on the fiftieth anniversary of my birth, I would again give my heart to God. In 1872 I I had seen the light in the darkness; this time I beheld and recognized it in its peculiar beauty, even while the sun was pouring out his own rays of brilliancy all around me. I resolved to give God my heart on the 10th of July; and I had a good excuse for putting it off two days, for I desired, for sentimental reasons, to commence living right again exactly on the day of my fiftieth anniversary. It is not wise to unnecessarily put things off, and, in this instance procrastination proved to be as great a thief as ever.

On the 10th, the day I was to have reformed and to have given my life to God, I happened to be very busy, and failed to comply with the vow I had solemnly made on the 8th, and it was not long before I had good reason to regret it; for on the 12th, two days afterward, I met with an accident that came near costing me my life. I spent the day and night of the 11th in Dumas, the nearest town, where I had gone for my mail. On the following day, the

12th, I went back to the ranch, and in some manner accidently shot myself through the leg, and came near bleeding to death before assistance reached me. While crawling on the ground, with blood spurting from an ugly wound, I thought of the resolution I had made four days before to lead a different life.

"Is this God's manner of punishing me for my negligence?" I asked myself; but I did not believe it was, and dismissed the thought from my mind. I feared, however, that my time had come, and I dreaded to think that I was to die by my own hand. In my helplessness I looked up to God and prayed to Him, with all the earnestness of my heart:

"O, God, I know I do not deserve to live, but, Merciful Father, grant me a few more years on this earth, so that I can serve you the rest of the days of my life. If, however, it is Your will that I die now, I shall accept my fate with resignation and calmness, realizing that Thou art the All-wise God and know best what to do with me."

God spared my life, and ever since then I have tried to live as I thought He would have me to do.

LIII

I SHOOT MYSELF

During the twelve years that I served the people of Texas as a State ranger I was exposed to hundreds of bullets and other dangers, but never received a serious injury until I shot myself, while guarding the LX and Turkey Track ranch in the summer of 1901, which fact I mentioned in the preceding chapter. After coming out of so many tight places unharmed, it seems remarkable to me that it should be left to my own hand to inflict the wound that crippled me for life.

I returned on the 12th day of July to my ranch, after spending the previous day and night in Dumas, and while passing through the pasture on my way to my ranch, my attention was attracted by the barking of a dog, the bawling of the cows, and the bleating of calves. A certain dog in the neighborhood had a habit of chasing the cattle away from the water, and, knowing this, I soon guessed the cause of the confusion and decided to kill the troublesome little canine. When the dog saw me, however, he ran away, going as fast as he could up the hill, with me close behind. I shot at him three times before he reached the top of a hill, and cocked my gun to have it ready for the fourth shot. Still after the dog, I was running my horse down the other side of a steep hill, when my saddle, which had been too loosely girted, slipped from the animal's back down to his neck. My horse, being a little wild, become frightened at this occurrence and commenced to jump and pitch considerably. I was still in the saddle, and while trying to control the horse I accidentally pulled the trigger of my sixshooter, which, as I have stated before, was cocked. That was an unlucky moment for me when I touched that trigger and discharged that gun, and the next few hours meant horrible pain and suffering, while the following days and weeks were but little better.

The bullet passed through my thigh, breaking the bone, and causing the blood to flow freely from the wound. I fell from the saddle to the ground and saw my horse turn and run up the hill. When I discovered that I had broken my leg, I pulled my boot off and began crawling, dragging the boot along with me. My boots were of extra fine quality, and I did not want to lose them; so after going about seventy-five yards I hid the boot in a place where I could easily find it afterwards.

Owing to the nature of the wound, I had to crawl backwards. A few moments after hiding the boot I fainted, and when I regained consciousness my fever was so high and my mouth was so parched with thirst that I crawled to a nearby creek.

The nearest house was two miles away, and, in trying to reach it, I crawled down this little stream. In quenching my awful thirst, I drank so much water that it cramped me. After four hours in the creek I took to the land, and tried to shorten my journey by crawling through the pasture. Some distance away from the creek I came upon a bunch of cattle. My leg was still bleeding, and the cattle, scenting the blood, came to me; I wished that they had been human beings. They did not know what to make of me, crawling along in such a strange manner, and becoming excited they walked around and around me in a circle, gazing at me all the while. Suddenly a big Durham bull, with sharp horns, advanced near me, and looked as if he was going to tear me up. About five steps from me he stopped and shook his head, pawed the earth and bellowed. I wished then that I had not lost my sixshooter when I fell from my horse a few hours before. I also remembered my Bill Cook Winchester, and thought about how quickly I would shoot this bull if I had it with me. As it was, I was defenseless, and expected every moment that the next would be my last. I could do nothing but talk to the beast, and I appealed to his principle, honor and mercy, and implored him not to attack me while I was so helpless. My prayer did not at first appear to have any effect on his mind and heart. While thus imploring the bull to go his way, I suddenly discovered that I had come upon a huge rattlesnake in his coil. I was within two feet of him when he began to use his rattles. I was satisfied from his movements that my time to die had at last arrived, and I felt rather creepish; but I managed to evade the snake by crawling around him, and thus ended my troubles of this nature.

The bull and the snake gone, I resumed my slow and painful journey. I had to travel by throwing my body backward with my good leg. At sundown I reached a barbed wire fence, and was almost famished for water, after my tedious crawl of an hour and a half across the pasture. Exhausted from loss of blood, I leaned my head against a post to rest. I soon became drowsy, however, and immediately roused myself to action; for I realized that to fall asleep then would mean death, as my leg continued to bleed and I was getting weaker all the while. Suddenly I heard the voice of a boy, and knew that someone was around. I was satisfied that it was Ray Bennett, the little son of the owner of the ranch, looking for his cows. I called out to him, but the wind was blowing toward me from his direction and I could not make him hear. The noise that the lad made while riding in that part of the pasture gradually died away, and I knew that he was gone. The hope that had suddenly leaped into my heart also departed, and left me in despair.

I was still suffering for water. I knew that there was an irrigation ditch about thirty yards on the other side of the fence, but getting to it was the problem. The fence was too low on the ground for me to crawl under, and climbing over it was, of course, out of the question. I thought of a place, however, about twenty yards further down, where the wind had blown the sand from under the fence and left a hole large enough for me to crawl under. I immediately made my way to that place and crawled through the hole. When I had got within fifteen yards of the ditch I looked up and saw the same little boy whom I had heard a short time before. I called him to me and asked him to bring me my hat full of water from the ditch. He not only brought mine but his own full, and I drank all the water that my hat would hold. The boy then summoned his father, who brought me stimulants and carried me in a wagon to his house. This part of the trip was easy for me, as Mr. Bennett had thoughtfully put a mattress and some quilts in the wagon, so I could rest more comfortably.

I asked Mr. Bennett to send me to my ranch, six miles away, but he would not think of it, saying that it was too far and that the trip would make against me. He sent for his wife, who happened to be at the creek fishing, and they went to lots of trouble and did everything possible to help me. My wound had swollen so that my clothing had to be cut off the injured leg. A fire was quickly made and a pot of coffee put on for me. Not wanting to occupy one of their best beds in my condition, I asked them to make a bed on the floor and let me lie there; but they would do nothing of the sort, and placed me in the best bed they had. I complained that I was too much trouble, but they assured me that I was not, and acted as if it were but a pleasure for them to do for me. Their manner and cordiality cheered me up, and made me feel at home. Such is rural hospitality and kindliness.

Mr. Bennett's oldest son, Charley, went to a line camp nearby and got Charley Smith, who lived there, to go thirty miles from the camp to a 'phone to summon Dr. Pearson at Amarillo, which place was twenty-five miles still further on. Dr. Pearson left Amarillo at two o'clock and reached me the next morning at eleven—about twenty-three hours after my accident. My leg was so badly swollen by that time that the doctor could do nothing but await developments.

I stayed at Mr. Bennett's six days and was treated royally. I shall never forget the kindness of that family. On Wednesday I was started in an ambulance to Amarillo, where I was to have my leg set. I was accompanied on my trip by five men, who carefully attended to my wants. A dozen men wanted to go with me, but I told them that five would be enough. When we reached our destination—the next day at noon—my friends in Amarillo met me and rendered me what assistance and comfort they could.

My leg had been broken so long that it could not be set straight. One end of the bone overlapped the other about three inches, which made a difficult operation for the surgeons.

I had to stay in Amarillo three months, but the kind ministrations of friends seemed to shorten the time and ameliorate my suffering. My experience was terrible, but while undergoing it, I was forcibly reminded of the fact that there are many people in the world who have real humanity in their hearts, and who possess much tender sympathy for those about them who fall victims to trouble and misfortune.

I was tendered financial assistance by the presidents of two banks of Amarillo, Messrs. W. H. Fuqua and Tol Ware, but, luckily, I did not need this assistance.

LIV

A CALL FOR PROTECTION

In 1891 I was ranching in Moore County, on the Canadian River. During that year I went to Dalhart, Dallam County, to visit some friends who had settled there. To get to Dalhart I had to go to Amarillo, which town was sixty miles from my ranch, and take the train there for Dalhart.

Dalhart was then a new town on the Rock Island, where that road intersects the Fort Worth & Denver. It was strictly a railroad town, and was located thirty-five miles south of Texline, the county seat. The town and county were supposed to be "prohibition," but two saloons and several gambling houses were running "wide open" in direct violation of the law.

These saloons were called "Tom Black" and "The Beckett," being named after their respective owners. The sheriff, who lived at Texline, had three deputies in Dalhart, but they were unable to put a stop to these violations of the law, and could not preserve peace and order. When I reached Dalhart things were in a bad shape, and a reign of terror existed. The town was filled with lawless people. Gambling was going on night and day, and drunkards were always to be seen staggering along the streets. A lady was not safe outside of her house. One lady was robbed in open daylight, and others were insulted by some of the low characters who daily emerged from the saloons, soaked with whiskey.

"Sullivan Wounded and in Peril."

While I was there on a visit, numbers of robberies occurred every night. The better element of the town were out-numbered by these outlaws, and were bluffed and scared by them. The lawlessness that reigned in Dalhart was becoming notorious, and the growth and the prosperity of the town was threatened. The people who were deeply concerned in the moral and material interests of the town realized that something had to be done with the outlaws and thugs who infested the city, and a committee of the best citizens of that place asked me to move to Dalhart and serve them as a peace officer. Justice of the Peace R. P. Edgel; Col. Oaks, the banker; Chapman, the real estate man, and Sheriff Morris and Col. Al Boyce were among those who asked me to help them break up the gang of outlaws who ruled their town. They offered me a hundred dollars a month for my services. I told them that it was a hard proposition to think about, as it was a bad bunch I would have to deal with, but I asked them for ten days time to think over their offer. They gave me the time I asked for, so I left at once for my ranch to attend to other business, and to think over their proposition.

Before the time limit expired, I decided to go to Dalhart and help the people out; so I got on my horse and rode across the country, it being sixty-five miles away, and reached Dalhart late in the evening. The sheriff met me, and I told him to "swear me in," which he did the next morning.

I knew that I would have to go about my business in a determined manner. I also realized that unless I was careful I would have lots of trouble on my hands. I went to work at once and billed twenty-seven cases against Tom Black for selling whiskey in a prohibition town and county, and eighteen cases against Beckett for the same offense. I also billed cases against Beckett's bartender and Tom Black's three bartenders. Black then employed a lawyer, a Mr. Smith of New Mexico, to represent him. Smith went to Sheriff Morris and told him that Black said that he would give him (Morris) fifty dollars if he would discharge me. Smith then remarked that Black could get along all right with the sheriff, but he could not stand me, and again asked Morris if he would not discharge me for that fifty dollars. The sheriff told him by no means would he "fire" me; that I was the only man he had ever had who did not stand in with the tough element. The sheriff told me later on about the proposition that the lawyer had made to him, but told me not to mention it, and I promised him I would not. When I met Black afterward, however, I was sorry I had made the promise, for I saw I had to break it. Black was coming down the street, and I called to him and rode into an alley to meet him.

I asked him if he had promised the sheriff fifty dollars if he would discharge me, and he answered that he had. I then asked him what his grievance was against me. He asked me if I did not summon the jury that indicted him in twenty-seven cases for selling whiskey. Of course I did not have anything to do with summoning the grand jury, and Black ought to have known better than to ask such a question. I told him that I summoned everyone of them, and asked him how he liked the men.

He said that they were the liars and damn thieves of the country, and I told him that he was one of those jump-backs himself.

At that time I was pulling off my gloves—I was not going to shoot Black; I was going to "throw down" on him, and make him listen to what I intended to say. Black thought that I was preparing to shoot him, as I afterward learned, so he made a spring and caught me around the waist pinioning my arms to my side. After scuffling for quite a while, I finally succeeded in getting my arm loose from his, and reached down and clutched his throat. I touched "White Man," my horse, with my left spur, and made him lean over toward Black. Black was jerking me all the time, and I still held to his throat. He finally twisted around until he got next to a porch, however, which gave him more power than I had while on my horse. My sixshooter had been working loosely on my belt, and his jerking me made it slip around in front of me. He suddenly loosened his hold on one side with his right hand and jerked my pistol from the scabbard. Black was a giant in size, weighing 225 pounds and measuring six feet and four inches in height.

I wondered for an instant what he was going to do with my sixshooter, but I soon saw; for after getting my gun he broke away from me and made a long run to his saloon, carrying the weapon with him.

My Winchester was at the butcher shop on the opposite side of the street from where the struggle went on, and while Black was running to his saloon I popped my spurs to my horse, and he reached the butcher shop in about three jumps. I called to Bob Troup to hand me my Winchester, which he did. I knew there were no cartridges in it, as I had taken all of them out for fear some thoughtless person would throw the lever and put a cartridge in the barrel, and not knowing how to get it out, and would let it go off and kill someone out in the street. I asked Troup then to hand me my belt, and, as he did so, I pulled two cartridges from it and loaded my rifle.

I was just whirling my house around to fire at Black, who was then entering the rear of his saloon, when I saw his half brother running toward me with my sixshooter. I stopped and waited for him, and when he got to me he said that Tom had sent my gun back to me. I told him to tell Tom that I had no intention of killing him, and that if he would behave himself I would never have to hurt him.

That night I watched Black's saloon, it being full of gamblers, robbers and thugs. While watching the saloon from the outside, I saw two men walk in and come out in a few minutes. I arrested them, and, searching them, I found on the person of each man a quart of whiskey. I escorted the two men to the office of the justice of the peace and sent for the justice. When he arrived at his office I made the two men swear under oath where they bought the whiskey, how much they paid for it, and from whom they purchased it. I then got two warrants out for Black, and getting Sheriff Morris to join me I went back to arrest him. Black learned that we were after him, however, and left the saloon and tried to make his escape. Several officers joined in the hunt, and we pursued him vigorously.

Sheriff Morris and Officer Logan went northeast down the Rock Island track to the depot, while Bill Garrett and I went northwest.

Pretty soon I saw a man running on the outer edge of the town, and saw him stop suddenly and lie down. I said to Bill Garrett, "That is Black." As we started after him, he got up and ran to a small building nearby.

When I had gotten within twenty-five yards of the house, and was facing the door, Black called out and asked if I was Sullivan.

I told him, "Yes."

Then he asked me if it was the sheriff with me.

I told him, "No;" that it was Bill Garrett. Then I told him to come out of the house and surrender.

He said: "Sullivan, I will surrender, but do not shoot me nor hurt me."

I replied that I would not hurt a hair on his head for the world if he did not make a play; "but if you do make a bad break," I added, "I will cut you off at your pockets."

He gave up quietly, and I took him to the office of the justice of the peace, where I could get a light and read the warrant to him. I shackled him then, and carried him on the next train to Texline, where he was lodged in the county jail. He remained there nine days and nights before he gave bond and was released. I met him soon after he gained his freedom, and had a long talk with him. He told me that he dreaded to be arrested by me that night, on account of the fight which we had engaged in the day before his arrest. Black wound up his side of the conversation by saying, "Sullivan, after what has happened between us, I shall always give you credit for being an honest officer. My respect for you has caused me to resolve to hereafter lead a different life. I know that I have been violating the law, but I will quit now, and I would like for you to knock out all the indictments which you have secured against me, and I will take oath that I will never sell another drop of whiskey in the State of Texas."

I saw the sheriff and district attorney and begged them to let him take the oath. I expected them to do so, but they did not agree with me, and persisted in prosecuting him. Black lived in Dalhart for quite awhile after I left there, and was assassinated by someone who shot him from across the street. The next sheriff—Jno. Webb—and his son were alleged to have committed the deed, and were tried, but acquitted. No one knew for certain who did the shooting.

Beckett and his bartender took the oath that Black wanted to take and went to Montana and I never heard from them again.

LV

UNKNOWN VICTIM FALLS IN A GUN FIGHT AT DALHART

"DECEMBER 22, 1901.

"TO OFFICER,

"DALHART, TEXAS:

"Arrest and hold one Tom Mayers for murder, as he has no examination, and notify sheriff at Beaver City, O. T. Thomas Mayers and Al Zimmerman left last night to get their money. You can find them at the Rock Island office in the morning at Dalhart. Both of these men are about twenty-eight years of age and they wear a beard of three weeks growth. Five feet five inches tall. Both wearing caps. Zimmerman accessory to murder.

"G. O. NEAL,

"Section Boss."

While in Dalhart I received the above telegram from Mr. Neal, who was working on the railroad about forty miles out of the city. The message was handed to me while I was talking to some railroad officials in the depot. I immediately wired Sheriff Morris to come down to Dalhart in the morning, telling him I wanted to see him on business.

Fearing that the sheriff was not in Texline and could not come down to help me, I deputized a Mr. McCormack to assist me in the case. I told the sheriff and McCormack, both, to come to a certain house before daylight.

Both men arrived at the house the next morning, on time, as I had requested, and I told them that we would go down to the depot before daybreak, so we would not be seen. I did not want anybody to know that anything was wrong. After reaching the depot, we went upstairs into the cashier's office and concealed ourselves.

When the cashier arrived at his office we told him what we were up there for, and I gave him the names of the two men who were to come for their money. "When they present their cards," I told him, "I want you to notify me."

He assured me that he would, and we lay still and waited for Mayers and his partner to show up.

About nine o'clock the sheriff went down stairs and stayed away quite awhile. When he returned I told him that he ought to stay with us, as the men might discover him hanging around the depot, and think something was "up" and not come in. The sheriff stayed with me then until eleven thirty o'clock and left me again. I suppose he grew impatient and thought the men were not coming.

Soon after the sheriff left, the cashier came to me and informed me that my men were at the window. Motioning McCormack to follow me, I opened the door that led into the hallway. I noticed that there were eight or nine men in the chute that led to the cashier's window. Every time a man looked in my direction I motioned him to come out.

In that manner I finally got everybody out, except the two men who were next to the window, and I wanted them to stay where they were.

They were watching the cashier and did not look around until I took the man nearest me by surprise and ordered him to hold his hands up. Hearing my command he whirled around quickly on his heels, and, as he did so, I twice again said, "hands up." When he saw McCormack and me with our pistols pointing at him, he ran his right hand down into his vest on the left side, and, as he did that, I fired, and so did McCormack. We shot at him, and the firing of our pistols created such a dense smoke in the little chute that we could not tell whether the man had a gun or not, and when we saw he was advancing toward us, we fired again, hitting him twice in the breast. Mayers was in front of him, and Zimmerman happened to be out in the hall, but I didn't know it then, and thought that the man who ran his hand down into his vest and advanced on us was one of them, and McCormack and I, both, fired at him. McCormack shot three times and I fired four times.

After being mortally shot, the victim of our guns ran out of the chute into the hallway, where he soon died from his wounds.

Mayers and Zimmerman both emptied their pistols at me, but only succeeded in hitting the man who had already received his fatal wounds. They shot him in the left ear, in the back, and in the right side. A shot struck Mayers in the chin, cutting the underpart of it off. The top of his sleeve was also torn by a stray bullet from Zimmerman's gun.

Before the fight was over, the smoke had become so dense in the chute and hallway that we had great difficulty in recognizing each other. During the confusion McCormack got on the other side of the room and came near shooting me, while firing at the man.

The man who was killed fell with both feet propped against the facing of the door that led into the cashier's room. I went to him when the smoke cleared away, and found at his left side a .44 cartridge and at his right side a .41 Colt's cartridge that had been snapped, the cap having gone two-thirds of the way in. His pistol had failed to shoot, and the smoke caused me not to see it. I looked around for his gun, but not finding it, I was satisfied that whoever pulled the dead man out of the door had taken it.

I stepped back to McCormack and told him that we had better knock the empties out and reload our guns as we had one more man to catch. When I learned that the wrong man had been killed, however, I knew that we had both the murderers to capture, and McCormack and I soon got busy.

Zimmerman and Mayers were running around in a cluster of excited men, but we picked them out, and gave chase to Zimmerman, leaving Mayers behind. The sheriff came up about that time, and I secured a horse for him and sent him after Zimmerman, who was trying very hard to make his escape. Then I summoned seventy-five men to help me search for Mayers, who I thought was hiding behind one of the numerous piles of culverts, ties and rails that were stacked in different places up and down the tracks.

Zimmerman was soon caught by the sheriff and brought back to me. A lady saw Zimmerman and Mayers drop two sixshooters in a barrel, and she got the weapons and sent them to me a little while after they were captured.

Mayers was found, after a three hours search, in a restaurant, bleeding to death from the wound on his chin, which he had received during the fight. I took him to a doctor and had him treated. Then I wired the sheriff at Beaver City, Oklahoma, that I had his men. He came at once and got them.

An inquest was held over the body of the man whom we had killed, and we were exonerated. The grand jury met in June, and they also declared that I was not guilty of murder. They were of the opinion that if the man had not been a fugitive from justice, he would not have tried to pull a gun on me. They further declared that I did what any other officer should have done under the same circumstances.

APPENDIX.

A Last Farewell.

Composed and Written by Dora Brown, October 13, 1902.

Just one year ago today, love,
  We said our last good-bye;
We parted in a quarrel—
  You know the reason why.
But that is all forgiven,
  And I dreamed it o'er and o'er;
Little did we think when parting,
  That we'd meet again no more.

Yes, it is all forgiven,
  A thousand times and more.
Oh, could it once more happen,
  To be forgiven o'er.
But it seems that our paths have parted,
  That the hope we have cherished must die—
Your looks and actions are remembered,
  Even your saying good-bye.

The world is full of pleasures,
  But few if any I see,
Since the one I loved so dearly
  Is taken away from me.
My prayers are for a brighter day,
  When we may prove our love,
But if we meet no more on earth,
  I hope we'll meet above.

Yes, I had rather share your grief
  Than other people's glee.
While you are nothing to the world,
  You are all the world to me.
I once saw sunshine in your smiles,
  Heard music in your tone;
I oft recall your words of love
  When I am all alone.

Once you were my betrothed,
  Noble, brave and true;
The love that gleamed in your brown eyes
  Was as gentle as the dew.
As fearless as our patriots,
  Who have braved the storms of sea,
You have roamed the West all over
  With a heart that beat for me.

Then you were a gay cowboy,
  Your life was happy and free;
There was nothing then to blight your joys,
  And pleasure was in store for me.
We vowed to wed and never part,
  The wedding day was set;
On Christmas night with hand and heart
  Our vows we'd plight, to ne'er regret.

But cruel fate has on us frowned,
  My prayers were all in vain;
My darling in the sentence found
  Seven long years to remain.
At Fowler in a convict camp
  My loved one toils each day,
While one at home with bleeding heart
  For him dost watch and pray.

The saloon at Dalhart caused this war;
  The man was not to blame.
For in this business we all know,
  Many men are brought to shame.
Don't let this hurt your feelings, love,
  And blame me not, my own dear Ed;
For all will be forgotten here
  When we are numbered with the dead.

My motto is, I will be true,
  My vows will never change;
I love none half so well as you,
  As long as life remains.
No other love my heart can wake,
  No matter where I rove,
The promise I shall never break—
  I am going to prove true to the one I love.

This July 12, 1908.

I knew this lady well. She used to live in Hutchinson county, Texas. She composed this poem for Ed while living in Channing, Texas, and sent it to him while he was in the penitentiary. W. J. L. SULLIVAN.

TEXAS RANGERS AFTER THE MOB.

Governor Culberson, from among the rest,
Chose four Rangers, whom he thought best.
He ordered us to San Saba to put down crime—
We met in Goldthwaite, all on time.
Two from the Panhandle, two from the Rio Grande,
Which made a jolly little Ranger band.

We stopped at a hotel to stay all night.
From what the people said, we expected a fight.
They puffed and blowed, and said we were in danger,
For a bushwhacker didn't like a Ranger.
We laughed at such talk, and considered it fun;
But wherever we went, we carried our gun.

We had a sixshooter, a Winchester, too,
That would shoot a buffalo through and through.
Next morning at early dawn,
We were off to San Saba, "as sure as you're born."
In a wagon, with sheet and bows,
How we stood it, the good Lord knows.

The roads were rough as rough could be—
Why it did not kill us, I cannot see.
Over mountains and hills, through the dust,
Over rocks, till I thought die I must.
We stopped in San Saba all that night,
Still expecting a hard little fight.

We rose next morning, gathered up our tricks,
Our camping outfit we began to fix.
We got a pair of mules, and a wagon, too—
Cooking utensils, and something to chew.
We wanted a cook, for we expected to be slain,
So the job was given to Buck Chamberlain.

We stopped in town a day or two.
Met some of the girls, as pretty as ever we knew.
Then to the Colorado River we soon did go.
When to return we did not know.
The sheriff went along to pilot us through.
He knew the country—Buck did, too.

We stopped at noon; got something to eat.
For economy, Buck was hard to beat.
He got on the wagon, taking a chew,
And said, "Come on, boys; better go through."
He drove into the creek his lines all slack,
Stalled his mules, and then looked back.

Sullivan, Barker and Edgar Neal,
All jumped off and grabbed a wheel.
Maddox jumped off and grabbed one, too.
Buck hit old Jack, and yelled, "Get up, Sue!"
We made it to the River, and pitched our tent;
To have a mess of fish we were all bent.

Still we were hearing a lot of the mob,
But we felt as though we were onto our job.
We rode over the country, went where we pleased,
But kept our eyes on all the big trees.
So we sent to Sheriff Bell, for a good watch-dog,
It would tickle you to death to see him catch a hog.

He caught by the tail, dropped down behind—
They went over that hill simply flying.
Here are the Texas Rangers, I know it is a hard life;
You had better find a girl and ask her to be your wife.
Now, if you trust in God, He will carry you through.
So good-bye, Ranger boys, I'll bid you adieu.

Composed by Allen Maddox, Co. D., Rio Grande; W. J. L. Sullivan, Sergt. Co. B., Panhandle.

January 11, 1897.

THE COWBOY'S HYMN.

When I think of the last great round-up
  On the eve of eternity's dawn,
I think of the host of the cowboys
  That have been with us here and have gone.

I think of those big-hearted fellows,
  Who'll divide with you blanket and bread,
With a piece of stray beef well roasted,
  And charge for it never a red.

I wonder if any will greet me
  On the sands of that evergreen shore,
With a hearty God bless you, old fellow,
  That you've met with so often before.

And I often look upward and wonder
  If the green fields will seem half so fair
If any the wrong trail have taken
  And fail to be over there.

The trail that leads down to perdition
  Is paved all the way with good deeds,
But in the great round-up of ages,
  Dear boys, this won't answer your needs.

The trail to green pastures, tho' narrow,
  Leads straight to the home in the sky,
And Jesus will give you your passport
  To the land in the sweet by and by.

Jesus has taken the contract
  To deliver all those who believe,
At the headquarters ranch of the Father,
  In the great range where none can deceive.

The inspector will stand at the gateway
  Where the herd, one and all, must go by,
And the round-up by the angels in judgment
  Must pass 'neath his all-searching eye.

No maverick nor slicks will be tallied
  In that great book of life in His home,
For He knows all the brands and the ear-marks
  That down thro' all ages have come.

But along with the strays and the sleepers
  The tailings must turn from the gate,
No road brand to give them admission,
  But that awful sad cry, "Too late!"

But I trust in that last great round-up,
  When the rider shall cut the big herd,
That the cowboy will be represented
  In the ear-mark and brand of the Lord.

To be shipped to that bright, mystic region
  Over there in green pastures to lie,
And lead by the crystal still waters
  To the home in the sweet by and by.

CHARLIE ROBERTS.

HUNTSVILLE GRAVEYARD.

There's an upland field near the Huntsville stream,
  Where the grass grows rank and tall.
A place of dread to cherished hearts
  When the evening shadows fall.
The laugh is hushed, the voice grows mute,
  It is passed with a quickened tread—
That little spot on God's green earth
  Where lies the convict dead.

How many lives that have promised fair
In boyhood's early prime
Have found their resting place up there,
That's marked with those of crime?
God grant that in their former days
They have done some deeds of love
That will balance all their erring ways
In the book of life above.

There's many a boy that has gone astray,
Yes, many a mother's pride,
And among the dead are laid away
On Huntsville's green hillside.
They perhaps are listening for his steps
That in death are forever still,
And watching for the form that lies
In Huntsville's graveyard hill.

Composed by A. E. Hillin, Clayton, New Mexico, July 1?, 1908.

I, W. J. Sullivan, caught this man in Dalhart while stationed there holding down crime.

SONG BALLAD OF THE DYING RANGER.

The sun was sinking in the west,
And fell with a lingering ray
Through the branches of the forest
Where the dying Ranger lay.
Beneath the shade of a palmetto,
And the silvery sunset sky,
Far away from his home in Texas,
We laid him down to die.

A group that gathered around him,
  His comrades in the fight,
The tears rolled down each manly cheek
  As they bid him a last good-night.
One friend, a loved companion,
  Was kneeling by his side,
Striving to quench the life-blood flow,
  But alas, in vain he tried.

His heart was filled with anguish,
  When he found it all in vain,
As over each loved companion's cheeks
  The tears rolled down like rain.
Up spoke the dying Ranger,
  Saying, "Weep no more for me;
I am crossing over the river,
  Where all beyond is free.

"Come, gather close around me,
  And listen to what I say;
I am going to tell a story
  While my spirit hastes away.
Far away in loved old Texas,
  That good old Lone Star State,
There is one that will wait my coming,
  With a weary heart she will wait.

"A fair young girl, my sister,
  My only hope and pride,
My only care from childhood,
  I have none else beside.
I've nourished and I've cherished,
  Her lonesome heart to cheer,
She loves, oh, so fondly,
  And she is to me so dear.

When our country was in danger
  And called for volunteers,
Sister threw her arms around me
  And bursted into tears.
Saying, 'Go, my darling brother,
  Drive the Indians from our shore.
My heart shall need your presence,
  But our country needs you more.'

"My mother, she lies sleeping
  Beneath the churchyard sod,
And many a year has passed and gone
  Since her spirit went to God.
My father lies perished
  Beneath the dark blue sea.
I've no father, I've no mother,
  There is only Nell and me.

"I know I love my country,
  I have given to her my all,
And had it not been for my sister,
  I would be content to fall.
I am dying, comrades, dying,
  She will see me never more,
But in vain she will wait my coming
  At the little cottage door.

"Come, gather close around me,
  And listen to my dying prayer.
You will be to her a brother,
  And shield with a brother's care?"
The Rangers spoke together,
  As one voice seemed to fall,
"She will be to us a sister,
  We will guard her, one and all."

One short, brief look of anguish
  O'er his youthful face was spread;
One quick, repulsive shadow,
  And the Ranger boy was dead.
On the banks of the old Nueces
  We laid him down to rest,
With a saddle for a pillow,
  And a Lone Star on his breast.

July 29, 1897. W. R. STILES.

THE OLD COWBOY OF THE PLAINS.

Written by a Mountain Buffalo Hunter—Jim Williams.

The day is bleak and cold and drear,
Summer is gone and winter is near;
The cold blue air upholds no birds,
And the cattle drift south in rustling herds.

The cowboy's round-up and trail work's done,
He hangs up his saddle, his spurs, and his gun,
He turns out his ponies on the mesquite grass,
And rustles the shippers for a homeward pass.
If he can't get a pass he will rustle the freights
Until he gets back to his home in the States.

He crossed the broad plains way back in '68,
When mules and ox-wagons hauled all the freight;
The California route was the usual trail,
And the stage coach and ponies carried the mail.
He would tell tales all winter of the long, long ago,
Of Indians on the prairies, and the herds of buffalo.

When you hear him sing his songs all so sad,
You'd think after all—he is not so bad.
"It's bury me not in the lone prairie,

Where the wild coyotes will howl o'er me,
Where the wild rose blooms, and the wind sports free,
Oh, bury me not on the lone prairie."

Then again he would laugh and fill with mirth,
And tell of Broncho that quits the earth,
Or when he was called out in the dead hour of night
To check a stampede, or Indians to fight.

From Texas to Montana he followed the trail,
And at Denver and Cheyenne he expected his mail.
None but old cowboy can realize or ever know
The dangers and hardships we experienced from South Texas
to mountain peaks of snow.
Through blinding rain and sunshine—though the days and
nights were long,
The weeks and months were rolling while he sung his cow-
boy song.
Trail on, Dogies, Montana is your home,
From the salt grass and cactus to the north plains you must
roam.

With his saddle for a pillow under his head,
The grass of the prairie served him for his bed.
Often he watched the bright stars until almost day,
Thinking of his home and sweetheart so far away.
He rejoices when frost falls, and he sees the Autumn moon,
For his work is about over, and he is going home soon.

He said to the boys as he boarded the train,
"You will never see me on the plains again.
This cowboy life is tough and all too sad.
I'll buy me a farm and settle down beside my old dad.
Just think of the big red apples, and my brown-eyed Sue,
And the good times that's coming to me down in old
'Missou.'"

He arrives home for Christmas, or perhaps Thanksgiving day,
When the old folks are happy, and the young folks are gay.
The girls are all smiling on reckless broncho rider,
And are treating him to home-made candy, ginger-cakes, and apple cider.
While one old couple were pleased, they were saying "Now, daughter Marandy,
We know very well for whom you are making that 'lasses' candy.
I wouldn't go to any trouble for him if I were you,
For he is desperately in love with your little cousin Sue."

So winter after winter the boys drifted home from the West,
And each girl in her linsey done her level best
To corral the wild cowboy and tame him down
And keep him from getting drunk and shooting up the town.
These boys seemed restless, and loved to chase the "Long Horn,"
Instead of being a nester and plowing the green corn.

He took in the theaters, the varieties and dance,
And took a sly drink whenever there was a chance.
He would seldom go home for his dinner at noon,
For he was watching some game in a down town saloon.
And on bologna, cheese and crackers he would feed,
While he told some tenderfoot of a big stampede.
His money all spent, he barely escapes jail,
And resolves once more to hit the cowboy trail.

Many years have passed, now, and the old folks are dead,
He don't go home winters, but is a line rider instead.
So alone in his dug-out through the long winter nights he does stay,
Listening to the wail of the winds, and the wolves on the hills not far away.

Quietly and slowly he is filling his pipe with long green
And thinking of the trials and hardships he has seen.
It's strange he did not save up some of his gains before it
was too late,
And buy that little farm back in his old native State;
For his girl sure loved him, and for him would still be
setting baits,
If it had not been for a young farmer back in the States.
So sadly and slowly he thinks as he smokes,
And is wondering who is now telling the tenderfoot's jokes.

He had been a Texas Ranger, and stood for many a year,
A target for desperadoes without a thought of fear.
Spring opens at last on the far distant plain,
And the line rider comes out in his saddle again.
He is dashing and bold, but he is getting quite old,
And the story of another cowboy will soon be told.
And as he lay on the ground and gazed at the same bright
stars in June,
He felt that his time was coming soon
To join the old cowboys who had gone before
To the great Eternal Round-up on the other shore.
His life had been wrecked, and he felt that he must soon die,
And he wondered if there was a home for the cowboys in
the Sweet By-and-By.
And if on the other side of Jordan in the green fields of Eden,
Where the Tree of Life is blooming—if there is rest for me.

"I have rode my last broncho," to the boys he had said,
While out on the prairie he made down his bed.
Alas, it was too true, for just before dawn
To the great Eternal Round-up his spirit had gone.
Then we dug a shallow grave, just six by three,
And buried him out on the lone prairie.

J. R. WILLIAMS.

HOUSE OF REPRESENTATIVES,
STATE OF TEXAS.

WHEREAS, Captain W. J. L. Sullivan was elected doorkeeper of the Thirty-First Legislature, at the beginning of the Regular Session, and has served in that capacity with distinction, and

WHEREAS, He has always been on time, and has never been absent from duty during the entire session, and

WHEREAS, During all the calls of the House he was always courteous, but firm as the "Rock of Gibraltar," and

WHEREAS, He has performed all the duties of Doorkeeper in a most efficient manner, therefore be it

Resolved, By the House of Representatives that the House extends to him its sincere thanks for so faithfully discharging all of his duties as Doorkeeper.

(Signed) ASTON.

DISTRICT CLERK'S OFFICE, TARRANT COUNTY.

W. D. MCVEAN, Clerk,
MIKE E. SMITH, Judge, 17th Dist.
IRBY DUNKLIN, Judge, 48th Dist.

FT. WORTH, TEXAS, January 9, 1902.

W. J. L. Sullivan, Esq., Dalhart, Texas.

MY DEAR FRIEND: I am in receipt of your letter of recent date telling me of the unfortunate occurence which resulted in the death of a man at your hands in your attempt to make an arrest of another. I had also read of the affair in the newspapers, and was much grieved to learn of it, both on your account as well as on account of the one who was killed. I have known you well ever since I was a child, and feel assured beyond the possibility of a doubt that the killing was an honest mistake on your part. I have never heard you charged of doing any living person a wilful wrong, and knowing your noble, generous nature as I do, I know you are incapable of such an act. Your brave, honest nature would not permit you to take even an unfair advantage of an enemy in a conflict, much less to wilfully kill an innocent man whom you did not know and against whom you had no grievance. While the affair was most unfortunate and deeply to be deplored, I have no doubt but that any officer in your position at the time, and viewing the surroundings as you did, would have done likewise. I consider the whole occurrence more as an accident, or as the result of accidental circumstances, than otherwise, and I sincerely sympathize with you in your deep regrets over it all. No one who knows and believes in you, as I do, will censure you under all the circumstances.

Your friend sincerely,
IRBY DUNKLIN.

LAST LETTER WRITTEN BY CONDEMNED MAN.

On October 27, 1899, Rev. G. E. Morrison was hanged in Vernon for the murder of his wife in Panhandle City in the spring of that year. This was one of the most celebrated and remarkable murders, trials and executions that has ever occurred in Texas, and attracted more attention, perhaps, in the State and Indian Territory than any case for many years, owing to the character and profession of the man. Captain John L. Sullivan, now of the Capitol police force, assisted in the execution of Morrison at Vernon, October 27, 1899. On the night previous, Captain Sullivan, who was on the death watch, requested the condemned man to write him a note that he might preserve it as a remembrance. He indited the following letter, which has never before been published, the original of which Captain Sullivan has in his possession:

"VERNON, TEXAS, October 26, 1899.

"*Mr. Sullivan.*

"DEAR SIR: You have asked me to write something that you can keep to remember the occasion of our meeting. I don't know what to say to you, but I hope the following may be entirely satisfactory:

"First, I believe in a future life, and I believe that men are punished for the sins of this life and are rewarded for the good things. Second, I believe in a general judgment and all must stand in that day before the bar of God and be judged. I believe I have the witness of God's spirit bearing witness with my own spirit, and believe that, though God allows man's law to take my life, yet he saves me, and I have no fears of the future whatever.

"Now, good-bye, and may you ever be the champion of the right and an enemy of the wrong.

"Your well wisher,

"G. E. MORRISON."

A TRIBUTE OF HONOR.

ABERDEEN, TEXAS, August 18, 1893.

At a meeting of our citizens today the following resolutions were adopted:

WHEREAS, On or about April 1, 1893, Corporal W. J. L. Sullivan, of Company B, Texas State Rangers, established headquarters in our midst to investigate charges of cattle stealing and other lawlessness preferred by certain private individuals, whose object in calling on the State for Rangers we believe to have been the intimidation of settlers; and

WHEREAS, Corporal Sullivan, upon coming here had a one-sided story and the prejudice of our people against him, and might very easily have precipated much trouble, but by his cool-headed, careful and thorough investigation, conducted in a gentlemanly manner, he succeeded in tracing these false accusations against our community to their source, and by his diplomacy averted trouble; and

WHEREAS, Corporal Sullivan has been recalled; now, therefore, be it

Resolved, That we, the undersigned citizens of Aberdeen, desire to thank Corporal Sullivan for his manly treatment of us all, and for his valuable services to our community while located here; and be it

Resolved, That we recommend Corporal Sullivan to his superior officer as an officer we believe to be possessed of the necessary nerve and ability to perform the most difficult task in his line, and one well calculated to make the ranger force respected and popular among the people; and be it further

Resolved, That these resolutions be sent to Corporal Sullivan, and that a copy of the same be furnished the following papers for publication: *Fort Worth Gazette*, *Quanah Chief*, *Amarillo Northwest* and *Memphis Herald*.

E. E. McCOLLISTER,	AWEN DILLARD,
W. A. DETHERAGE,	J. G. WRIGHT,
J. R. HILL,	S. L. BLAKE,
S. F. BOOKER,	J. A. McCRACKEN,
T. E. WALKER.	J. H. WHITE,
T. O. JONES,	BOB BROWN,
J. N. JONES,	D. A. GOODWIN,
M. C. STARKEY,	ANDY JONES,
WM. WALL,	J. W. AMMONS.
S. E. TOMLINSON,	J. C. WALKER,
T. E. WALKER,	T. B. STARKEY,
WM. JONES,	A. L. WALKER,
W. E. JOHNSON,	W. P. BUMPASS.

I hewed to the line and let the chips fall where they may and won the victory. Thank God my motto is do right and go ahead.

W. J. L. SULLIVAN,
Ex-Sergeant of Company B, Texas Rangers.

(Copied August 23, 1906, by G. C. Morriss.)

(Copy.)

AUSTIN, TEXAS, August 1, 1906.

Sergeant W. J. L. Sullivan, City.

MY DEAR FELLOW: I am glad to bear testimony to the brave and faithful service you rendered your State as a Texas Ranger during a long series of years of arduous duties. I know you love Texas far more than thousands who have proclaimed their patriotism from political platforms.

I have not forgotten the dark days of ten to twenty years ago when, in many localities, the presence of the Texas Rangers was the only thing that gave hope of protection of life and property; the years of awful dread that hung over the counties bordering on the Colorado River, from Milburn to Bluffton, which saw the first rift in the lowering clouds of mob rule, when you and your little band of rangers "struck camp" in the very heart of the "mob country," and by fearless vigilance, absolutely untiring, day and night, at last brought assurance of law and order to that terror-stricken community.

It was my privilege to see much of you in that dangerous position and undertaking, and my pleasure to know that the courage, tact and skill displayed by you under many trying conditions met with the praise of all fair-minded citizens. And, too, I was a distressed onlooker and interested with painful regret the unfortunate accident that befell you one cold December day in 1896, resulting from your extreme desire to lend every aid to the county authorities in ferreting out crime. The sheriff rushed up to you saying: "John L., let one of your boys go after Del Dean, a horse thief, who has just left town. He was indicted by the grand jury." There were none of your "boys" in hailing distance, so you said "What's the matter with me" and was now chasing that coyote through the mountain brakes south of the town, where "Old Sorrel" made an airship of you and your ordnance of dynamite shells in an unannounced rehearsal of a "high somersaulting performance," I suppose, although I had not noticed any bill-posters about town that day. During the "rehearsal" you went on a strike, two strikes in fact, one for high air and then for a soft spot to alight, which was about a solid acre of "honeycomb" limestone, where the citizens' committee of lawyers and doctors spent several hours tenderly, and with suppressed curses, gathered up the fragments and carting them to town. There were no rocks left on that acre, you and the dynamite cartridges had not done a thing to them.

I think you still carry a souvenir of that performance somewhere about your right wrist. You merit the gratitude of every friend of law and order, by your long, courageous, faithful service as a Texas Ranger of the true type, ever ready, never tiring, and always civil, courteous and sober. Texas never had a more zealous and fearless ranger in her service, is the way I size you up, and this is endorsed by hundreds of men scattered from here to the lonely dugout in the Indian Territory, where Beckham passed in his checks one bitter cold night when "Old John L.," far in the van, grew impatient for the others to arrive, and charged the outlaws. You carry a broken rib, I believe, as a memento of that little fracas. Your friend,

SIDON HARRIS.

TURNER AND BOYCE,
Lawyers.

AMARILLO, TEXAS, December 26, 1904.

To the Members-elect of the Twenty-ninth Legislature:

It has just come to my knowledge that Mr. W. J. L. Sullivan, late of Company B, Frontier Battalion of Texas, will be an applicant for the position of Doorkeeper of the House of Representatives, and, as a citizen of Texas who feels a deep interest in securing the very best material to fill the various places of public trust, I wish to add my testimony to the deserving worth of Mr. Sullivan.

I have known Mr. Sullivan for over fifteen years, during a large portion of which time he was stationed at Amarillo as one of the rangers of Company B, and, if my memory is not at fault, he was for some time First Sergeant of that company here. He has always been one of the most zealous and faithful officers it has ever been my pleasure to know. He was always unflinching in his high regard for and devotion to duty. It is his nature to be passionately loyal to the enforcement of the laws, and so well-known is his courage and fidelity to duty that his name has long been a constant terror to evil-doers. His fearlessness in the face of danger, and his sterling integrity was, during his stay with us, a reassuring safeguard of our protection against violators of the law. No matter how desperate the criminal whose capture was desired, nor how many hardships were to be endured in his pursuit, there was never the slightest degree of hesitancy on the part of Mr. Sullivan, or "John

L.," as he is familiarly known. He was always ready and anxious to do his whole duty, and his valuable services have been highly beneficial to the Panhandle.

Besides being a splendid officer, Mr. Sullivan is a sober, honorable and reliable man. He stands high among the people who know him best, and he has many friends throughout this section who feel that his long and faithful services to the State, the many hardships which he endured, and the example which he set for the public good, ought to be rewarded now with the position which he seeks.

Very truly yours,

THOS. F. TURNER.

SAN SABA, TEXAS, January 25, 1902.

To the Grand Jury of Dallam County, Texas, at their next regular session in and for said county:

I have learned with regret of the trouble my old friend, John L. Sullivan, has had recently in your county in trying to arrest two murderers, which he had been notified and requested to do, and, knowing John L. as I do, and feeling the interest in him and his welfare that I do, and having good reasons for it that I have, I hope you will excuse me for writing on the subject, which is not done to try and influence you corruptly or wrongfully, but that you consider his character and disposition along with the actions you may deem necessary to investigate and take action on, in connection with the unfortunate affair John L. got into, and that you may do your duty and act justly in the matter.

I have known Mr. Sullivan for the last ten or twelve years as an officer and law-abiding citizen, and State ranger as a man that is always ready to try to do his duty fearlessly. I was District Attorney in the Forty-sixth Judicial District of Texas under G. A. Brown, the District Judge, and in some of the counties in my district I had some just such characters to deal with in my prosecutions as those murderers Sullivan ran onto in your country, and they would form clans to try to intimidate and deter me from prosecuting them vigorously, and my District Judge often deemed it necessary to call on the Governor for State rangers to come to the courts for my protection and safety. John L. Sullivan was always sent as sergeant of a squad of rangers to protect me and preserve order in the court, and John L. always accomplished the purpose for which he was sent, and did it wisely and fearlessly, and proved himself one of the best and most cautious, as well as determined, officers I ever saw or knew. He has come in contact with such daring, desperate characters so often, and knows their plays so well, that he can't afford to wait, when he sees a criminal make an obstinate play, when he is trying to arrest him, and the question in this case, as it seems, was whether he should wait and delay his opportunity until him or his assistant, or both, were shot down by the outlaws; or, whether as a good officer, he should do his duty at once, and out of the abundance of caution beat his desired prisoners shooting, when the first intimation of the outlaws indicated their purpose, and in the furore and excitement, and so many shooting on both sides—one to enforce the majesty of the law and the other to resist it—it is hard to tell whose bullets did the killing. All good citizens should uphold the majesty of the law and the officers of the law in the discharge of their duty.

I am not dictating to you, Gentlemen, but I do not want you to be deceived in the character of Mr. Sullivan. Begging your pardon for troubling you this much, I am truly yours for justice and right, be that in favor or against my old friend.

(Signed) G. W. WALTERS,
Attorney-at-Law.

DALHART, TEXAS, January 12, 1903.

To Whom it May Concern:

I take pleasure in pleading the cause of my old friend, John L. Sullivan. I have known him long, and know him to be a brave, good man and a Christian gentleman. Long he has served in Western Texas. He has spent the best part of his life in its service, always ready to defend the right and fight the wrong. I have seen, in new Western towns—even right here in Dalhart, in its infancy—robberies and lawlessness of all kinds committed daily.

John L. Sullivan came, and it was like a calm before a mighty storm, wrestling with unseen danger, but he was there calm and immovable, brave as a lion, ready to do his duty and serve his people. And now, dear friends, I think he deserves something at the hands of the people he has served so long and faithfully. Long live my old friend and his name long after he is gone. "Honor to whom honor is due" has always been my motto.

There is no man in Western Texas more deserving than John L. Sullivan, the faithful discharger of duty.

Respectfully,
(Signed) MRS. M. S. JACKSON.

FLACK & DALRYMPLE,
ATTORNEYS-AT-LAW.

LLANO, TEXAS, July 29, 1907.

To Governor Geo. Curry, Santa Fe, N. M.

MY DEAR SIR: I take great pleasure in recommending to your most favorable consideration my old friend, Capt. W. J. L. Sullivan; I understand he will be an applicant for a captaincy of mounted police under your administration; if so, you can find no better man for the position. I have known him as an officer for the past twenty-five years, and when I say he has at all times done his full duty I speak only the truth, and when it can be said of a man that he has faithfully discharged his duty, no more need be said, for in that sentence is contained sufficient to a business man like yourself; however, I will further say that Capt. Sullivan has been with a Texas Ranger force for the past twelve years, and in that capacity he has been called to the aid of our peace officers from one end of our State to the other. His field of action has been mostly confined to West Texas, where he has had to contend with all character of violators of the law, from the midnight assassin to the petty thief, but his best work has been done in dealing with what is known in central West Texas as the "mob;" I speak of this because his work in that line came under my direct observation. In ridding that portion of our State of the "mob" Texas owes Capt. Sullivan a debt of gratitude she can never pay. He is a man of great executive ability, nature having done much for him in that way; cool, calm and deliberate in action, and in whose make-up the word "fear" has no abiding place "in any fiber of his existence." During his long career as an officer he has been called to face danger in its every form, and he has yet to show the "white feather," for he has never done so up to this hour. Having been brought frequently "face to face" with the very worst element of the West Texas desperado, he has never come in contact with a sufficient number to check him from his duty. He has courage without rashness, and his experience as an officer would aid him greatly in dealing with the character of men you want controlled; he knows them as few men know them; he knows the best method of dealing with them, and I am sure he would make you a valuable man anywhere you may place him.

My dear sir, in writing you as I have, in behalf of Capt. Sullivan, I have not indulged in fulsome praise, but simply speak truthful words which came direct from my heart. I have not gone into detail, because I know your time is too valuable to be thus consumed. Myself, in common with a host of Capt. Sullivan's friends out West, would be much pleased if you could find it consistent with your duty to give him a place under your administration; he is worthy of it, and I feel sure you would never have cause to regret it. Captain Sullivan's personal integrity is above reproach, and his courage is unsurpassed.

Hoping your administration will prove a blessing to your people, and with best regards, I am,

Yours very respectfully,
(Signed) JAS. FLACK,
Ex-Member Texas Legislature (not Thirtieth.)

DALHART, TEXAS, January 8, 1903.

To Whom it May Concern:

I am very much pleased to write this letter in behalf of our much appreciated friend, Mr. John L. Sullivan. If, perchance, it may through some divine power or influence, find its way to a deserving community who needs and is able to pay for the services of a faithful, much deserving officer and Christian gentleman, which we Dalhart people have found in the person of Mr. Sullivan. His presence in our midst is like a ray of sunshine in time of storm, both as a firm, kind-spoken officer—whom he thinks would feel sadly disgraced should he for a moment shrink from his duty or betray any trust reposed in him—and a friendly Christian visitor. We regret very much to lose him from our little town, which he served so faithfully.

His memory, I dare say, will be like letters of gold in pictures of silver when we think of the reformation wrought by his services, and wherever he may go we bid him God speed.

Very truly,
(Signed) MRS. S. HOFFMAN.

DOUGLASSVILLE, TEXAS, February 13, 1908.

Gov. George Curry, Santa Fe, N. M.

DEAR SIR: I am now about to engage in a duty that we owe to each other, our fellow man; I am now recommending to you a friend, a man that I know to be true to his country and true to his fellow man in every sense of the word. The man that I present to you is the Hon. W. J. L. Sullivan; I have known him for forty years. He is an honorable, truthful, sober Christian gentleman as ever lived, and if you can help Mr. Sullivan I will appreciate the favor, and he has many friends in this country that will consider it a great favor.

Yours truly,

(Signed) W. B. HEATH,

Justice of the Peace, Cass County, Texas.

DOUGLASSVILLE, TEXAS, February 9, 1908.

Gov. George Curry, Santa Fe, N. M.

DEAR SIR: The gentleman who presents this to you is Capt. W. J. L. Sullivan, a citizen of this place, who visits your city on personal business, and any courtesies shown him will be gratefully appreciated by his many friends throughout Texas.

For many years he has served our State as one of the Rangers, and in other responsible ways, and has always been true to every trust and faithful and honest to every friend, and a terror to evildoers. Hence, it is, I take pleasure in handing you this indorsement of an honest man.

Respectfully yours,

(Signed) W. D. STONE.

DOUGLASSVILLE, TEXAS, February 14, 1908.
Gov. George Curry, Santa Fe, N. M.

DEAR SIR: I take this occasion to introduce to you the bearer of this letter, Mr. W. J. L. Sullivan, whom I have known personally for forty years. Mr. Sullivan is generous, honorable, and, in fact, one of Nature's noblemen.

He served in the capacity of State Ranger for twelve years, with great credit to himself and an honor to the State of Texas. Mr. Sullivan visits your State on private business.

Any advice and assistance you may render will be highly appreciated by him, and duly acknowledged by myself.

Believing that your acquaintance will be mutual and agreeable, I am,

Very respectfully,
(Signed) T. G. HOWE, M. D.

February 5, 1908.
Gov. George Curry, Santa Fe, N. M.

DEAR SIR: This will introduce to your favorable acquaintance my friend, Mr. W. J. L. Sullivan, whom I have favorably known for more than thirty-five years. Mr. Sullivan has been an officer as State Ranger for twelve years, in which position he rendered efficient and a valuable service to our State.

I can truthfully say that Mr. Sullivan is a truthful, reliable, sober gentleman, and stands pre-eminently high with all Texans as an officer and public servant.

My friend, Sullivan, visits your State on private

business of his own. Anything that you can do for him, or favors rendered, will be highly appreciated by the writer.

Very respectfully,
(Signed) A. C. SMITH.

DOUGLASSVILLE, TEXAS, February 13, 1908.

Gov. George Curry, Santa Fe, N. M.

DEAR SIR: This will be handed to you by my friend, Mr. W. J. L. Sullivan, whom I have known from his boyhood, and cheerfully recommend him to the favorable consideration and confidence of the public.

Any favors shown him will be duly appreciated by his many friends in Cass County, Texas.

Yours respectfully,
(Signed) A. C. OLIVER, M. D.

THE EX-RANGER RECOVERING.

A BRAVE AND FEARLESS MAN WHO HAS TAKEN MANY RISKS.

Ex-Ranger Sergeant W. J. L. Sullivan (better known as "John L.") is rapidly improving from the recent accident which occurred at his ranch north of town some two months ago. As a full account was given in these columns at the time, it is not necessary to refer to it again.

Sullivan's first experience as a ranger was in 1888, under Captain McMurry, who was then commanding Company B of the State Ranger force. Since that time Sullivan has been a terror to the lawbreakers of the State and has succeeded in running down more criminals than any other Ranger ever in the service, before or since.

Eminently possessed of those sturdy qualities which go to make up a successful executive officer, Sullivan has justly earned a distinction as broad as that State, which he so faithfully served.

Quiet, cool, and always sober, he stood when in the service without a peer in the State as an executive officer. He made some enemies, it is true, but so has every other officer who has discharged his duty as honestly and as fearlessly as he did. It is not necessary to enumerate numerous scouts and various expeditions led and the important captures made, as they are a part of the criminal annals of our State. Wish you an immediate recovery, John L., and may you live many years to rest on the laurels you have so justly won.—*Amarillo Northwest.*